BANKER'S RACKET OR CONSUMER BENEFIT?
A Consumer View of the Single European Market for Financial Services

About the Author

Jeremy Mitchell is a Consumer Policy Adviser to international organisations, governments, public bodies and consumer groups on banking and financial services, telecommunications and broadcasting issues. Current and recent assignments include projects with the Organisation for Economic Co-operation and Development (Paris), European Commission (Brussels), Netherlands Ministry of Economic Affairs, New Zealand Ministry of Consumer Affairs, Australian Telecommunications Commission and Rhode Island Consumers' Council (USA). Jeremy Mitchell broadcasts frequently on radio and television and has published widely on consumer issues. His previous Policy Studies Institute report was on *Electronic Banking and the Consumer – the European Dimension* (1988). Other recent books and monographs that he has written or edited include *Money and the Consumer – a Consumer View of the Financial Services Revolution* (1988), *Access to Basic Banking Services – the Problems of Low-income American Consumers* (1990), *The Consumer and Financial Services – New Horizons* (1990) and (with Claire Milne) *Quality of Service Indicators for the Telephone Service to Residential Consumers* (1990).

Previous UK posts that Jeremy Mitchell has held include Deputy Research Director and Director of Information at Consumers' Association, Assistant Secretary at the National Economic Development Office, Secretary and Chief Executive of the Social Science Research Council, Director of Consumer Affairs at the Office of Fair Trading and – for nine years until end-1986 – Director of the National Consumer Council. He currently holds a number of appointments on UK self-regulatory bodies, including the Independent Committee for the Supervision of Telephone Information Services, the Direct Mail Services Standards Board and the Life Assurance and Unit Trust Regulatory Organisation Monitoring Committee. Jeremy Mitchell is also a member of the European Commission's Payment Systems Users' Liaison Group.

BANKER'S RACKET OR CONSUMER BENEFIT?

A Consumer View of the Single European Market for Financial Services

Jeremy Mitchell

Policy Studies Institute

PUBLISHING

The publishing imprint of the independent
POLICY STUDIES INSTITUTE
100 Park Village East, London NW1 3SR
Telephone: 071–387 2171; Fax: 071–388 0914

ISBN 0 85374 512 9

PSI Report 722

A CIP catalogue record of this book is available from the British Library.

1 2 3 4 5 6 7 8 9

How to obtain PSI publications
All bookshop and individual orders should be sent to PSI's distributors:

BEBC Ltd
9 Albion Close, Parkstone, Poole, Dorset, BH12 2LL

Books will normally be despatched in 24 hours. Cheques should be made
payable to BEBC Ltd.

Credit card and telephone/fax orders may be placed on the following UK
freephone numbers:

FREEPHONE: 0800 262260 FREEFAX: 0800 262266

Booktrade representation (UK & Eire)
Book Representation Ltd
PO Box 17, Canvey Island, Essex SS8 8HZ

PSI Subscriptions
PSI Publications are available on subscription.
Further information from PSI's subscription agent:

Carfax Publishing Company Ltd
Abingdon Science Park, PO Box 25, Abingdon OX14 3UE

Typeset by Stanford Desktop Publishing Services, Milton Keynes
Printed in Great Britain by Billing and Sons Ltd, Worcester

Contents

Introduction

The Europe of '1992' is taking shape in front of our eyes. Many of the details remain to be filled in, but the main outlines can be discerned even now. We can already see the barriers to the free movement of goods, services and labour between the member countries of the Community falling away. Frontiers between nation states in the EC will remain – for the present, at least – to mark political and cultural boundaries, but there will be a single European market extending throughout all twelve member countries.

This report examines one aspect of the Europe of 1992, the single market for banking, insurance and other financial services. It is not the first time that this subject has been studied. There have been extensive public and private debates about the impact that the single market for financial services will have on banks in country A or insurers in country B. There has been much speculation about how the financial services industry in Europe will match up against its counterparts in the US and Japan.

In all these discussions, there has been one conspicuous gap – the impact that the single market for financial services will have on the individual consumer. Apart from an occasional ritual genuflection in the direction of the consumer's interest, there has been no attempt either by the governments of member states or by the European Commission itself to make a systematic assessment of how the individual consumer will be affected. This is a serious defect. Unless the single market benefits individual consumers, the massive effort which is going in to restructuring the legal and regulatory framework for banking, insurance and other financial services will have been a waste of time and money.

This report draws up a balance sheet of the pros and cons for individual consumers throughout the EC. It weighs the prospective

1

benefits of wider choice and lower prices against the possible weakening of consumer protection. There are separate chapters devoted to the Commission's overall strategy, banking, borrowing money, payment cards, cross-border payments, insurance, saving and investing and protecting personal financial information. The conclusions of the report point to gaps in the Commission's proposals which need to be filled if consumers are to gain the greatest possible benefit from the changes that are taking place.

I owe a great deal to the many consumer leaders, bankers, lawyers and others with whom I have discussed my ideas over the last two years. I would in particular like to thank Peter Troberg (European Commission DG XV), Jean Allix and Patrick Latham (European Commission Consumer Policy Service), Bob Schmitz (formerly of BEUC), Thierry Bourgoignie (University of Louvain-la-Neuve), Bernd Stauder (University of Geneva), Joop Koopman (Netherlands Ministry of Economic Affairs) and Norbert Reich (University of Bremen) for the information and stimulus they have provided – though they are in no way responsible for any deficiencies. My thanks are also due to Dominic Mitchell of Solo Publishing Ltd. for his editorial assistance and to Lynette Davidson, who prepared the index. Janet Powney gave me enthusiastic encouragement and help thoughout the preparation of this report.

I am grateful to American Express Foundation for a grant to carry out this work and particularly to Meredith Layer, Julian Oliver and James Tobin (American Express Company) for their support. Policy Studies Institute have given me every help in carrying out the study and publishing the report. The views expressed are mine and are not necessarily shared by American Express Foundation or Policy Studies Institute.

Jeremy Mitchell
London, September 1991

The Grand Design

A Greek building a house near Salonika gets a life-insurance linked mortgage from a British building society. An Italian living in Milan obtains a personal loan from a German bank. A Copenhagen-based Dane is issued with a credit card by a French bank. Are these scenarios even remotely probable in the post-1992 European Community or will they stay in the realms of fantasy? Much of the political debate about the single market for financial services focuses on the impact that it might have on the different sectors of the financial services industry – which companies will win, which will lose. Relatively little attention has been paid to the effect it will have on consumers in the member countries of the Community.

How might individual consumers benefit from a single market in financial services? The benefits could come from lower prices, stemming from increased competition and efficiency, and from a wider choice of different kinds of financial service and a wider choice of banks and other financial institutions. That is the theory. This report sets out to examine how the theory might work out in practice and to draw up a consumer balance sheet of the revolutionary changes that are taking place on the initiative of the European Commission. However, what is happening in financial services needs to be set in the context of the Commission's wider objectives in building a single market.

The New Approach
The idea of setting up a single European market for goods and services has its origins in the formation of the Community, as set out in the Treaty of Rome of 1957. The Treaty envisaged the establishment of a single, EC-wide integrated market, free from restrictions on the movement of people, goods, services and capital. It also laid down the

3

principles of competition policy to prevent market distortions and provided for the approximation of relevant laws and indirect taxation.

The early years saw attention being focused on a common customs tariff and on indirect taxation, culminating in the adoption of the sixth VAT (Value Added Tax) Directive in 1977. This was accompanied by a programme of harmonisation, designed to create sets of common rules on an EC-wide basis. Harmonisation was carried out under Article 100 of the Treaty of Rome, which gives the Council of Ministers power, when deciding unanimously on a proposal put forward by the Commission, to legislate by Directive for the approximation of the laws, regulations and administrative actions of member countries, in so far as they affect the establishment of the common market. Detailed harmonisation based on Article 100 has often proved to be a lengthy and cumbersome procedure, not least because it requires unanimity.

In 1985, the Commission launched a 'new approach' in the context of a White Paper (bafflingly coloured pink in its English language version) called *Completing the Internal Market* (European Commission 1985). This sets out a fresh strategy based on 'mutual recognition'. The principle on which this is based is that goods and services from one member country should be allowed free entry into other member countries. Each member country is obliged to recognise the relevant laws and regulations of all the others, subject only to the minimum necessary harmonisation. If a product or service meets the requirements of any one member country, there should be no restrictions on its sale throughout the EC. The White Paper also embodies a comprehensive programme for achieving a single European market within which there will be free movement of people, goods, services and capital. The target date for implementation is 31 December 1992.

The Commission's proposals were adopted by the Council of Ministers later in 1985 and commitment to achieving the single market by 31 December 1992 was included among the reforms to the Treaty of Rome known as the Single European Act (or Single Act). This was signed by all member states and ratified by national parliaments in 1986. Amongst other things, it lays down new procedures which speed up Community decision-making by extending majority voting to virtually all aspects of the single market programme.

The 'new approach' has been greeted with some anxiety by consumer organisations. The free circulation of goods and services throughout the Community appears to override national consumer protection measures, unless it can be shown that these are in the general good. Also, many new approach Directives do not seem to include any harmonisation of minimum levels of consumer protection on an EC-wide basis (European Consumer Law Group 1990).

Financial Services

The earlier (that is, pre-1985) phase of the common market programme saw much more progress in relation to the movement of goods across internal frontiers than on the freedom to provide services. However, the White Paper puts considerable emphasis on the whole range of services, because '... it is no exaggeration to see the establishment of a common market in services as one of the main preconditions for a return to economic prosperity.' Within the service sector, financial services are picked out as being of prime importance, as they provide the infrastructure for so many other areas of the economy. The importance of financial services in the entire single market strategy has been emphasised by the Director General of DG XV of the Commission, responsible for financial institutions:

> 'Financial services play an increasingly important role in the economy of all Community countries. Confronted with an increasingly globally organised financial market, it is therefore essential that Europe becomes an efficient and liberal marketplace if it is not to lose business and the market that goes with it. From the consumer's point of view it is important that he or she should have access to a wide range of competitive financial products irrespective of country of origin. Last but not least, financial services are an important input for the rest of the Community's economy. It is essential for our manufacturing sector's competitiveness that our financial services sector should be as competitive as possible. European industry has to be able to finance itself on the finest possible terms and buy its insurance as cheaply as possible.' (Fitchew 1988)

How does the Commission propose to deploy its new strategy to achieve a single market in financial services? There are three main components:

- Free flow of money across the Community's internal frontiers. Member countries are committed to the abolition of all remaining controls on capital movements within the Community, qualified only by short-term concessions to enable governments to deal with economic crises;
- Freedom of financial institutions that are authorised in any one Community country to establish themselves wherever they wish throughout the twelve member countries without having to seek

5

separate authorisation. This 'passport' approach is being developed in relation to banking, insurance and investment services;
• Freedom of EC-based financial institutions to sell their services across internal Community frontiers.

As has been pointed out above, the intention is that this new framework for financial services markets should bring benefits to consumers in the form of lower prices and a wider choice of financial institutions and services. These should be the result of increased international competition and the removal of market distortions – not least those caused by differing forms of government intervention from country to country and widely different regulatory regimes. Until now, financial services markets in a number of EC countries have been wholly or partly sheltered from international competition by restrictions on the movement of capital and on the entry of foreign firms.

One of the Commission's explicit objectives is to sweep away these barriers and so enable consumers to have a wider choice. An indirect outcome of more vigorous international competition should be the weakening or abandonment of domestic cartels in some financial services markets, which have often operated with outright or tacit government approval.

Price Differences
What is the scope for reduction in the prices paid by consumers for retail financial services? There seem to be wide divergences in current price levels between countries. A study for the Cecchini Report on *The Cost of Non-Europe in Financial Services* (Price Waterhouse 1988) reveals big variations in the price to consumers of loans, credit cards, home mortgages, running a bank account, term insurance, home and motor insurance, and charges for investing in securities.

For example, there are major differences between countries in the cost of operating a bank account:

	Annual cost of typical current cheque account
Belgium	nil
Netherlands	nil
Spain	2 ECU
Luxembourg	8 ECU
France	10 ECU
UK	112 ECU
Germany	117 ECU
Italy	240 ECU

Another study shows that the annual fee for a Visa credit card ranges from nil for some Visa cards in the UK, through 15 ECU in France and 20 ECU in Italy, up to 60 ECU in Germany (Battelle 1989).

For personal loans, a French study points to wide differences in margins between money-market refinancing costs and the interest rates that banks charge consumers (Association Française des Banques 1987):

	Banks' personal loan margins
France	4–10%
Germany	7–11%
Spain	7–12%
UK	13–14%
Italy	18–23%

In the life insurance market, a comparison of term insurance premiums in Community countries discloses huge variations. The annual premiums for a 10-year term policy (for a 30-year-old male smoker, with cover of 100,000 ECU) vary between countries by a ratio of about ten to one, out of all proportion to any possible differences in risk (BEUC 1988):

	Term insurance annual premiums
UK	88–123 ECU
Ireland	129–235 ECU
Netherlands	164–228 ECU
Denmark	230 ECU
Germany	252–285 ECU
Spain	257–526 ECU
France	276–300 ECU
Belgium	325–334 ECU
Luxembourg	334 ECU
Italy	373 ECU
Greece	480–496 ECU
Portugal	900 ECU

As an example of differences in returns on savings, the Belgian consumer group *Test Achats* has reported that British, French and Italian consumers putting their pounds sterling, francs or lire respectively into term accounts would get a higher rate of interest from Netherlands banks than from banks in their own countries.

These illustrations of variations in the prices of retail financial services between Community countries show the potential for price reductions in a fully competitive single market, if the Commission's initiatives really succeed in giving consumers the opportunity of choosing in an EC-wide market. What prospects are there for consumers that these and the benefits arising from greater choice will be realised in practice? What constraints exist and what are the chances of overcoming them?

Barriers to the Single Market for Financial Services

The constraints on the development of a fully open and competitive single European market for retail financial services are of three kinds:

- Differences in the 'culture' of retail financial services between Community countries;
- Continuing government intervention in retail financial markets and divergences in the legal and regulatory frameworks for financial institutions;
- Strategies adopted by financial institutions to limit competition and to preserve insulated national markets.

The significance of these three types of constraint is examined in the rest of this chapter.

Other Markets, Other Cultures

Cultural distinctions between national retail financial markets within the European Community are both extensive and profound. The growing internationalisation of the markets for corporate financial services has not yet generally percolated through to retail level. Choice of payment modes is an obvious example. Consumers in France, the UK and Italy are heavy users of cheques for non-cash payments, and low users of bank transfers. Conversely, Dutch and German consumers write few cheques, but use bank transfers for over half of their non-cash payments (*People and Payments* 1987: Battelle Institute 1991).

Even the technological revolution in the retail delivery of financial services is taking place at very varying speeds in different Community countries. There are over 330 ATMs (Automated Teller Machines) per million population in Spain and over 230 per million in the UK and France, compared with around 150 per million or under in the remaining countries of the Community – as few as 15 ATMs per million population in Greece. The penetration of new banking technology seems to have little to do with the 'maturity' of retail financial markets: relative to population, Spain has three times as many ATMs as Germany (Battelle Institute 1990).

The use of different forms of credit also varies widely between countries. There are over 25 million bank and 10 million retailer credit cards in issue in the UK, compared with around three million in Germany. Fixed-rate interest loans are the norm for house purchase in Belgium, France, Germany, Italy and the Netherlands, while variable-rate mortgages dominate the UK housing market.

Consumers' savings preferences also show marked divergences. For example, less than 25 per cent of UK unit trust/mutual funds are not in equities, compared with some 75 per cent in Germany – and the proportion of French mutual funds in bonds and money market instruments is as high as 82 per cent. Yet there are profound differences between German and French consumers in their approach to mutual funds – German investors hold theirs on average for ten years while the French switch every three years (*Retail Banker International* 3 April 1989).

These cultural differences in the pattern of use of retail financial services between Community countries are the outcome of complex interaction between what financial institutions offer and what consumers prefer, within distinct national legal and regulatory frameworks. Sometimes, these differences reflect measurable variations in levels of income or occupational structures. In other instances, consumers may be influenced by long national folk memories of extreme currency depreciations, or institutional or stock market collapse.

It would be a mistake to think these differences are immutable. Recent history shows that consumers are prepared to change their habits if an innovation really meets their needs. The growing acceptance of ATMs – which make it much easier for consumers to get at their own money when and where they want it – is an example of how one specific aspect of the retail financial services scenario is being transformed within a few years.

Nevertheless, deeply embedded national patterns of use of retail financial services may well be generally slow to change and so, ironically, act as a brake on the allocation to individual consumers of any benefits stemming from the single market for financial services.

Government Intervention

Government intervention in financial services markets may be diminished by the arrival of the single European market but it is not going to disappear. This applies, though rather differently, to markets for both banking and insurance services. Banks are held by law, custom and the watchful eye of central banks to be 'special', in the sense that the normal rules of the market should not necessarily apply to them. This distinctiveness derives from banks' triple job of operating a national payments system, supplying an underlying source of liquidity for all other institutions and providing a 'gearbox' for monetary policy. While deregulation is in many countries widening the scope of competition in relation to prices and services, both among banks and between banks and other financial institutions, complex formal and informal structures which maintain the influence of governments and/or central banks over the banking system are likely to persist.

One powerful constraint on the free play of markets for retail banking services is the need for governments to maintain the stability and soundness of individual banks and of the banking system as a whole. In some countries, the armoury of techniques used extends well beyond prudential controls, which will in effect be aligned throughout the Community by the Directive on solvency ratios, examined in more detail below in the chapter on Banking. For example, while interest rate deregulation has been a feature of many national banking markets since the mid-1960s, four Community countries still retain official interest rate controls or approved agreements (Bröker 1989).

Other government-initiated or authorised limitations on banking competition affect fees and commissions, the permissible range of marketable financial instruments, the volume of credit and the terms on which it is supplied, and deposit reserve requirements. There are still considerable and varying restrictions in Community countries on the kinds of activities in which banks are allowed to engage, though the agreed definition of a common core of permitted banking activities in the Second Banking Directive (also examined in the chapter on Banking) will, when implemented, go some way to eliminating the anti-competitive effects of these imposed structural boundaries.

The reduction of government-inspired limitations on competition has even further to go in insurance than in banking. In a number of national insurance markets within the Community, perceived consumer protection needs override competitive considerations. Measures to control institutions' access to the market and their on-going activities are supplemented by regulatory controls over premiums, general and special contract conditions and a range of other matters directly affecting the consumer. In Germany, for example, tight regulatory controls over life insurance premiums and policy conditions shift competition to bonuses or dividends, while in Portugal minimum premiums are fixed by the regulatory authority. Some classes of insurance may be operated by the state, either as a monopoly or in competition with the private sector. In several member countries there are constraints either on taking out an insurance policy with a foreign insurer, or on taking out an insurance policy in a foreign currency, or both. In some, 'composite' insurers which transact both life and non-life insurance are prohibited. Partial or general exemption from national competition laws is widespread.

The European Commission's earlier efforts to break down these anti-competitive restrictions and create a single European market in insurance ran into considerable difficulties. Some governments of member countries have been tenacious in trying to preserve insulated national insurance markets. They have been unintentionally aided by judgments of the Court of Justice made in December 1986 in cases taken by the Commission against Germany, Ireland, France and Denmark (Court of Justice 1986). A key element in the Court's judgments was the qualified conclusion that member states may sometimes be justified in the interests of policyholder protection in restricting freedom to provide insurance services.

Seeking a way forward from this enigmatic set of judgments, Commissioner Sir Leon Brittan announced in November 1989 that new draft 'framework directives' would be put forward for life and non- life insurance, proposing that insurance companies should operate throughout the EC with a single licence. The implications of these are examined in the chapter on Insurance.

Another aspect of government intervention to prevent competition in both banking and insurance markets is the restriction of the activities of foreign financial institutions. This may take the form of barriers that prevent or inhibit the establishment of foreign financial institutions. These may range from outright prohibition through constraints on organisational form (for example, on setting up subsidiaries or branches) to restrictions on size (for example, the number of branches). Foreign financial institutions may be limited to certain functions and may be constrained from acquiring or taking a participating share in domestic institutions. There may be restrictions on the nationality of members of the board of directors.

There may also be discriminatory treatment against established foreign financial institutions. This may be deliberate (for example, a requirement that each branch should have specifically designated capital) or incidental, in the sense that legal or administrative requirements on both foreign and domestic financial institutions bear more heavily in practice on foreign ones.

The Move Towards Deregulation

To set against these examples of government intervention in financial markets, there is already a far-reaching pattern of changes in the government's role in financial markets in EC and many other developed countries. These changes largely precede the development of instruments by the Commission for achieving a single market. One of the key elements in the changes that are taking place is structural deregulation, intended to enable or encourage competition in financial services, or to strengthen the working of market forces, especially by the reduction or abolition of government involvement. The easing or abolition of controls over the pricing of financial services (especially, interest rates) is often also an important component of change. National regulatory reforms currently include the following:

- The partial or complete removal of structural boundaries between different types of financial institution, allowing them to compete with each other. For example, in the UK the Building Societies Act 1986 allows building societies much greater freedom to compete domestically with banks in providing consumers with a wide range of banking services, including unsecured loans. In Spain, savings banks have been allowed to carry out some of the same operations as banks since 1977 and there were similar changes in France in 1978 and Portugal in 1981;

- Changes in the criteria which financial institutions have to meet to be allowed to enter a market. These have recently been altered or are under review in a number of countries, especially in relation to making it easier for foreign institutions to enter – an aspect of liberalisation of financial markets referred to below;

- Changes in prudential control requirements intended either to stimulate competition without jeopardising institutional soundness or to align regulatory structures for different types of financial institution;

- Transference of publicly owned financial institutions to the private sector, for example Société Générale in France, National Girobank in the UK and Banco Fonsecas e Burnay and Banco Espirito Santo e Commercial de Lisboa in Portugal;

•   Liberalisation of entry for foreign financial institutions and the removal of restrictions on their activities.

These examples illustrate the impact that structural regulatory changes within EC member countries have already had – and will continue to have – on the providers and consumers of banking services. However, it should be noted that it is often the anti-competitive aspects of structural regulation which have been relaxed or abolished, with the aim of helping financial markets to function more effectively. Other aspects of regulation – for example, prudential controls over the capital adequacy and liquidity of financial institutions, have, if anything, been tightened up. Also, in some countries and some markets there has also been a strengthening of conduct regulation. A major example of this is the Financial Services Act 1986 in the UK, which provides a statutory framework for self-regulation by financial institutions carrying on investment business.

National regulatory systems are also changing in response to market and public policy pressures for regulatory alignment. Different regulatory standards for different types of financial institution may distort competition and it is now accepted in many countries that one policy objective should be to produce a 'level playing field' for all financial institutions which operate in any market. Regulatory convergence of this kind may in the long term lead to regulation by function rather than by type of institution, but for the present most national regulatory systems are still either institution-based or hybrid.

The current process of regulatory reform will not lead to a totally *un*regulated financial services sector. The use of the word 'deregulation' without substantial qualification can be misleading. However, with such major changes taking place, consumers may understandably be anxious that the consumer protection components of financial services regulation may be weakened or may disappear altogether in the upheaval. This continues to be a persistent theme in the approach of consumer organisations to the single market for financial services.

Commercial Policies
Whether or not individual consumers benefit in practice from the single market for financial services will also depend on how financial institutions respond to new competitive opportunities. It is already clear that there are considerable structural realignments in progress. A

13

number of defensive national mergers have taken place or are in prospect, intended to exploit economies of scale in the domestic market and to fight off possible competition from other Community countries – examples are the insurance merger of Compagnie du Midi with Axa in France and the banking mergers of Banco de Bilbao with Banco de Vizcaya and Banco Central with Banco Hispano Americano in Spain.

An example of a more offensive European strategy is evident in the expansion of Allianz, Germany and Europe's largest insurance company. Allianz is reported to have acquired a stake in Dresdner Bank, Germany's second largest bank, with a view to selling its services and products in some 600 Dresdner branches in five länder. Allianz is also reported to have a 24 per cent stake in Bayerische Hypotheken-und-Wechselbank and a 10 per cent stake in Bayerische Vereinsbank. It has a reciprocal 25 per cent stake in Münchener Ruckversichung, the world's biggest reinsurance company. In other Community countries, Allianz has bought Cornhill Insurance (UK) as well as majority shareholdings in Riunione Adriatica di Sicurita, Italy's second biggest insurance company, and Ercos, the Spanish insurer. Allianz also has major insurance interests in France. It appears to be bidding to become a pan-European financial services conglomerate, strong in both banking and insurance markets.

Germany's largest bank, Deutsche Bank, has acquired a branch network in Italy with its takeover of Banca d'America e d'Italia and has branches, offices or wholly owned subsidiaries in Belgium, France, Luxembourg, the Netherlands, Portugal and the UK. It has an affiliated company with a branch network in Portugal and maintains relationships with banks in Denmark, Greece and Ireland. In Spain, Deutsche Bank has a major stake in Banco Trans, which has 100 branches. However, it is reported to have abandoned plans to become a major retail bank in France.

A major French bank, Crédit Lyonnais, has a substantial stake in Credito Bergamasco (Italy). In Spain, it controls Banco Commercial Español, has bought Banco Jover and has an alliance with Banco Hispano Americano. It has acquired Chase Banque de Commerce in Belgium and Slavenburgs and Nederlandse Kredietbank in the Netherlands.

Pan-European strategies of this kind seem to be rare. Indeed, mergers and acquisitions may be a less frequently used single market strategy than joint ventures, networking agreements and other collaborative arrangements. For example, Abbey National, a bank that was until recently the UK's second largest building society, is embarking on small-scale joint ventures in the Italian and Spanish mortgage markets. France's largest privately owned bank, Société Générale, and largest specialist mortgage company, Crédit Foncier de France, have joined forces to launch Capital Home Loans in the UK, which will work with established distributors – though again the target of a £1 billion mortgage book within three years seems relatively modest.

However, direct inward competition of any kind is likely to be the exception rather than the rule. The scope for cross-border transactions in retail financial services is limited and the high cost of setting up branch networks from scratch inhibits the development of direct competition at retail level. Christopher Johnson of Lloyds Bank (UK) points out that 'Retail branch banking may be the most profitable and dynamic area for each major bank in its home territory, and yet the most difficult area for foreign banks to invade with success, and without heavy casualties.' It is not surprising that a study of the costs of establishment of financial institutions concludes that 'For those institutions seeking to establish in new territories the costs of doing so may mean a long payback period' (Price Waterhouse 1989).

As a result, whatever the future may hold, there is as yet relatively little international competition in most EC retail financial markets. For example, although the UK mortgage market has been one of the most open in the world since 1981, foreign lenders probably take no more than two or three per cent of it. While a number of UK insurance companies operate elsewhere in the EC, they again have no more than two or three per cent of the market, measured by premium income (House of Commons 1989).

In the short-term, financial institutions are likely to be primarily concerned with protecting themselves from the perceived threats of foreign takeover and inward competition. The emphasis is likely to be on defensive mergers and practices intended to preserve national retail markets in their present form with the minimum of structural and competitive change. Such practices generally work against the economic interests of individual consumers in that they minimise and delay the benefits that could accrue to them from the completion of the single market.

Effective competition policy at Community and national levels is therefore of prime importance if consumers are to secure any practical benefits from the single market for financial services. This is one of the issues examined in more detail in later chapters of this report.

Banking

The opportunity given to the consumer to open a bank account in any Community country, in any Community currency, is of little practical value unless it is underpinned by the freedom to transfer money without constraint across national boundaries. The same is true for the freedom of banks and other financial institutions to establish themselves in any EC member country or sell their services across frontiers. Many countries have had elaborate structures for restricting the flow of capital. While these have been wholly or partly dismantled in many countries – the UK, for example, abolished all controls in 1979 – they still constitute an impediment to Community-wide trade in banking and other financial services.

Liberalisation of Capital Movements

The abolition of all national restrictions on the free flow of money across the Community's internal frontiers is therefore a necessary condition for the full freedom of financial services within the EC. Without it, it would be impossible to make further substantial progress in liberalising Community trade in banking, insurance or investment services.

The EC's advance has come in four stages. First, in 1960 a Directive was adopted which classified capital into four categories, each subject to different degrees of liberalisation, based on a nomenclature of capital transactions. The most unconditional degree of liberalisation included direct investment, investment in property, personal capital movements, transfers in performance of insurance contracts and authors' royalties. In 1962, a second Directive was adopted clarifying and adding to the previous Directive. This still left major barriers to capital movement. The turning point was a change in French policy in the early 1980s, which made possible the adoption of the Third Capital Liberalisation

Directive (86/566/EEC) in 1986. This classified capital movements into three different categories – those subject to unconditional liberalisation, those on which a member state might keep exchange restrictions for economic policy reasons, and those on which member states were obliged to notify the Commission about restrictions in force.

This third Directive still left the EC some way short of full freedom of capital movements. Only Germany, the Netherlands and the UK had complete freedom. In Belgium and Luxembourg, freedom was qualified by a dual exchange rate system, with an 'official' foreign exchange market (involving only authorised banks) for current transactions and a 'free' one for capital movements. French consumers have not normally been allowed to hold bank accounts in other countries or to open foreign currency accounts in France. Italy has been engaged in lifting most remaining restrictions, with Italian consumers' freedom to hold lire or foreign currency deposits abroad being the last control. Denmark also retained some restrictions designed to inhibit capital outflows, while Ireland, Greece, Portugal and Spain have more widespread systems of exchange control which are currently being dismantled.

The fourth and final stage of liberalisation of capital movements has now started. In 1988, a Fourth Capital Liberalisation Directive (88/361/EEC) was adopted which commits member countries to the abolition of all remaining controls on capital movements within the EC and to policies aimed at the same objective so far as non-EC countries are concerned. The Directive came into effect for most member countries on 1 July 1990, with Ireland, Spain, Greece and Portugal being allowed until end-1992 – indeed, Greece and Portugal have a possible further three year extension after that.

The Directive is qualified by some concessions intended to help member countries deal with economic crises. There is a safeguard clause which allows temporary (up to six months) exchange controls on short term capital movements, subject to authorisation by the Commission and Council. This is meant for use only in circumstances when capital flows are of 'exceptional magnitude' and likely to lead to 'serious disturbances' in the conduct of monetary and exchange rate policies. Also, member countries may introduce measures to regulate bank liquidity, even if these constitute a restriction on capital movements, as long as such measures are accepted as being necessary.

The Directive was adopted despite the major reservations of France and Denmark, both fearful of capital outflows motivated by tax evasion. France asked for a clause in the Directive dealing with the harmonisation of tax rates for savings and portfolio investments, but this was rejected on the grounds that there should not be any structural link between freedom of capital movements and tax harmonisation. In the event, those countries that were most anxious that liberalisation of capital movements might lead to a haemorrhaging of their national capital have not seen their worst fears realised – outflows of capital have been much less than anticipated.

Another link that was rejected at the time (by the UK) was between freedom of capital movements and commitment to membership of the Exchange Rate Mechanism (ERM) of the European Monetary System (EMS). An accompanying text which read that 'the measures to liberalise ... the foreign exchanges ... will not take on their full significance and exert their full effects unless they are accompanied by parallel efforts to achieve the equal participation by 1992 of all the currencies in the Community in the Exchange Rate Mechanism of the European Monetary System' did not survive. However, the UK subsequently joined the ERM in 1990.

In the long-term, the 1988 Capital Liberalisation Directive may prove to be of fundamental importance in securing for consumers many of the benefits of a single European market in financial services. This is because it allows the freedom of those transactions which generate capital movements, including investment in property, loans and their repayment, buying and selling securities, opening current and deposit accounts, insurance contracts, gifts and inheritances. In theory, all prohibitions by member states which prevent consumers from buying financial services from other EC countries should go. Consumers should be able to open a bank account in any EC country, in any currency they choose. They should be able to take out an insurance contract in any member country.

Banking – First Moves
The 1977 First Banking Directive (77/780/EEC) removed some of the obstacles to free establishment for banks throughout the EC. In fact, the Directive covers 'credit institutions', financial institutions which both accept repayable deposits and grant credit. Central banks, Post Office giro institutions, municipal banks, credit unions and certain specialist institutions are excluded. In the UK, the term credit institutions includes banks and building societies. For convenience, the word bank is used here, unless there are provisions which are specific to building societies or other specialised types of credit institution.

The main purpose of this Directive is to lay down the conditions which must be met to enable a bank to begin operation. Member countries are no longer able to refuse banking licences to new banks or bank branches from other member states on grounds of economic need. The Directive also provides for the broad approximation of criteria for issuing bank licences and sets out a programme for establishing common criteria for monitoring solvency and liquidity. For example, to obtain a licence a bank must have:

- Separate capital from the resources of its proprietors;
- Meet an initial capital requirement test;
- Be directed by at least two persons of 'sufficient repute' and of 'sufficient experience'.

However, this first Directive leaves untouched three significant obstacles to the free establishment of banks and similar institutions throughout the Community. First, a bank that wants to set up a branch in another member state still has to be authorised by the host country. Second, what it can do in the host country is constrained by that country's supervisory authority. Third, in most member countries (but not the UK) branches of foreign banks have to be endowed with earmarked capital, as if they were separate banks. Also, the first Directive makes no provision for giving banks the freedom to supply banking services across borders within the EC.

Second Banking Directive

To fill these gaps and to provide a more comprehensive framework for a single market in banking services, the Second Banking Directive (89/646/EEC) was adopted in 1989. This is the cornerstone of the Commission's strategy for financial services and is a model for the changes that are being introduced in insurance and investment services. Its most important provision is that of a single banking licence – a 'passport' – which would allow a bank to operate throughout the EC. The licence would be issued by the home country's supervisory authority. It would not be necessary for a bank to seek separate authorisation in each of the 12 member states. The strategy of the Second Banking Directive is in line with the Commission's 'new approach', outlined in the previous chapter on The Grand Design. The date for implementation of the Directive is 1 January 1993.

The single licence would authorise a bank to carry out in all member states any of the banking activities on an agreed list, providing the activity was not prohibited in the bank's home country. The agreed list includes the following activities:

- Deposit-taking and other forms of borrowing;
- Lending, including consumer credit and mortgage lending;
- Financial leasing;
- Money transmission services;
- Issuing and administering means of payment – credit cards, traveller's cheques and banker's drafts;
- Guarantees and commitments;
- Trading for own account or account of customers in money market instruments, foreign exchange, financial futures and options, exchange and interest rate instruments and transferable securities;
- Participation in share issues;
- Advice to undertakings on capital structure etc.;
- Money broking;
- Portfolio management and advice;
- Safekeeping and administration of securities;
- Credit reference services;
- Safe custody services.

This list is a minimum. It is open to any national supervisory authority to authorise a bank to engage in other activities, but such 'unlisted' activities (for example, insurance broking) may be subject to host country control. The host country retains responsibility for supervising liquidity, in collaboration with the home country, and for the implementation of monetary policy, but may not discriminate in favour of its domestic banks.

With these exceptions, the principle of home country supervisory control is intended to be dominant. It will no longer be necessary for a bank to be separately authorised by a host country either to set up branches or to supply banking services on a cross-border basis. Such branches will not have to have separately endowed capital and separate branch accounts, though subsidiaries will be subject to host country authorisation and control of a non-discriminatory nature – that is, on the same basis as the authorisation and control procedures applied to the host country's own institutions.

From the principle of home country supervisory control, it follows that there must be some harmonisation of essential standards for tne prudential supervision of banks by national supervisory authorities and mutual recognition of the way in which each member country applies its standards. The prudential standards to be harmonised in this Directive are:

- Minimum authorised capital of 5 million ECU (which may be lower for certain kinds of credit institutions);
- Information on major shareholders;
- Limitations on a bank's holdings in non-financial institutions.

The Second Banking Directive is one of a troika of 'new approach' banking measures, the others being the Own Funds and Solvency Ratio Directives. The Own Funds Directive (89/299/EEC) is a technical measure which establishes common definitions and a classification system for the capital base of banks as a basis for setting minimum levels of capital adequacy.

The Solvency Ratio Directive (89/647/EEC) uses the definitions of the Own Funds Directive to set minimum standards of capital adequacy which EC banks have to meet, by establishing a uniform method of assessing the ability of credit institutions to meet credit losses arising from customer default. The provisions of this Directive are closely aligned with the Cooke Committee proposals for International Convergence of Capital Movement and Capital Standards (1988) drawn up by a committee of supervisory authorities under the auspices of the Bank of International Settlements, Basle. This agreement covers Japan, USA, Switzerland, Canada and Sweden, as well as some EC member states – the Group of 10 or G10.

Consumer Protection Safeguards

What are the consumer protection implications of the Second Banking Directive? Throughout the discussions of the various drafts of the Directive, consumer organisations have been concerned that the principle of home country control could drive a coach and horses through national consumer protection systems unless there was some degree of harmonisation of the standards of consumer protection throughout all member countries of the EC. The fear has been that an analogue of 'Gresham's Law' would operate, in that the levels of national consumer protection would be forced downwards to the lowest level prevailing in any member state (see for example Allix 1990).

This anxiety was well based while the Directive was going through its various drafts. However, the final text means that consumers' worst fears have not been realised. The crucial text lies in Article 21, which starts by setting out the procedures for dealing with banks which do not comply in the host state with legal provisions adopted pursuant to the Directive involving the power of the host country regulatory authorities. It then continues:

> 'The foregoing provisions shall not affect the power of host Member States to take appropriate measures to prevent or to punish irregularities committed within their territories which are contrary to the legal rules they have adopted in the interest of the general good. This shall include the possibility of preventing offending institutions from initiating any further transactions within their territories.' (Article 21(5))

This power of the host country to enforce its national laws and regulations is subject to appeal in the host country's courts.

The text of the Directive gives no guidance on the criteria to be used in determining 'the general good'. It is not clear whether it includes all aspects of consumer protection – or, if not, which. The matter is left to the courts to decide. However, it seems reasonable at this early stage to say that any host member country's laws and regulations which discriminate against banks from other member countries in the guise of consumer protection are unlikely to get through the 'general good' gateway.

Many member countries will undoubtedly be reviewing their national laws and regulations in the light of this aspect of the Directive. Consumer organisations need to be vigilant to make sure that genuine national consumer protection measures do not disappear along with discriminatory provisions. The situation after 1 January 1993, when the Second Banking Directive is implemented, will need to be monitored closely to see what developments occur. If consumer protection in relation to banking is jeopardised throughout the EC, as analysis of the Directive suggests it might be, then pressure will need to be applied to the Commission to take remedial action.

Potential Consumer Benefits from Competition

In theory, the Second Banking Directive will make it possible for there to be greatly intensified competition throughout the Community in providing banking services. The Commission's view is that it '... will certainly lead to a reduction in the cost of banking services' as well as widening consumer choice of banking services and institutions. The extent to which this increased competition might actually happen in practice has been discussed in the previous chapter on The Grand

Design. Whatever impact there is on services provided by banks to corporate customers, there are many who are sceptical about the positive benefits for individual consumers, certainly in the short-term. For example, in its examination of financial services and the single market, the UK House of Commons Trade and Industry Committee (1989) says that it does not expect there to be much effect on the supply of banking and other financial services at retail level '... for many years to come'. Consumer tastes, local conduct of business rules and the cost of establishing a local distribution network will all deter sudden expansion of retail services in the short-term. The Committee concludes that the main achievement of the single market programme will be to enhance the wholesale financial services business conducted at company level by established firms and to promote the wider international spread of financial conglomerates.

This is an understandably cautious view of the role that international competition stimulated by the single market might play in bringing benefits to consumers. It is reinforced by the fact that the primary objective of the Directive is to force governments to take steps to remove barriers to institutions from other member countries operating in their own country, rather than compel them to remove obstacles that prevent institutions based in their own countries from operating in others. In the UK, for example, building societies – defined as credit institutions under the Directive – are only allowed to operate outside the UK through subsidiaries which themselves have no power to lend or take deposits within the UK. The Second Banking Directive will not in itself change this, though there is a strong case for saying that continued legal restrictions of this kind in national law are contrary to the spirit, if not the letter, of the Directive (Building Societies Association 1990).

However, these reservations do not give sufficient attention to the changes that there will be to *national* retail banking markets in many EC countries. A key to this is the Annex to the Second Banking Directive, which lists (see above) those banking activities which are integral to banking and which come within the scope of mutual recognition. The list is appreciably wider than existing banking functions in some countries – for example, in France, banks may not engage in securities trading on the stock exchange, while in Greece, banks are forbidden to manage investment portfolios.

A number of national restrictions on what activities banks can engage in may therefore have to go, if these activities are defined as integral to banking in the Annex to the Directive. This will have the effect of pushing banks towards 'universal banking' – that is, providing a full range of banking services – not least as a defensive measure against possible competition from banks elsewhere in the EC. If there is any reduction in the price of banking services to consumers – and this cannot be taken for granted – it is more likely to come from intensified competition in deregulated national markets rather than from liberalisation as such. European consumers may well have to live with the paradox that the main impact of the Second Banking Directive will be to accelerate deregulation in national markets within the EC rather than to create a truly Community-wide market.

The Prospect for Prices

What are the prospects for lower prices of retail banking services in a single market? The study carried out by Price Waterhouse for the Commission compares the prices of specific banking services in member countries with the average of the four lowest member countries – the assumption being that competitive forces in a single market will tend to push down prices towards the lowest prevailing level. The table below shows the estimate of percentage differences in prices – for example, in Belgium the cost of consumer credit is 41 per cent below the average of the four lowest countries, while in France it is 105 per cent above. Note that the table includes some banking services not used by individual consumers, such as letters of credit and commercial loans. Finally, the bottom row in the table shows the overall potential price reduction for each country – for example, if the prices of banking services in Spain moved to the average of the four lowest countries in the EC, there would overall be a 15 per cent reduction.

Estimate of percentage differences in prices of banking services

	Bel	Fra	Ger	Itl	Lux	Nth	Spn	UK
Consumer credit	-41	105	136		-26	31	39	121
Credit cards	79	-30	60	89	-12	43	26	16
Mortgages	31	118	57	-4		-6	118	-20
Letters of credit	22	-7	-10	9	27	17	59	8
Foreign exchange	6	56	31	23	33	-46	196	16
Travellers' cheques	35	39	-7	22	-7	33	30	-7
Commercial loans	-5	-7	6	9	6	43	19	46
	Theoretical potential percentage price reduction							
All banking	15	25	33	18	16	10	34	18

(Price Waterhouse 1988)

The double impact if increased international competition in banking and increased national competition in less regulated markets may have some impact on reducing prices for banking services. However, there are doubts as to how effective competition will prove to be in practice (Dermine 1991). Also, any tendency for prices to move downwards as a result of competition may be swamped by the anxious search that banks are carrying out to find ways of increasing profits from their retail operations. Following their massive exposure to third world bad debt, many banks have in recent years badly over-reached themselves on corporate lending and are looking to retail banking to redress the balance. It is a new phenomenon that retail banking, which used to be the low status, neglected arm of banking, is now the cornerstone of profitability.

This has two specific consequences for consumers. First, despite competition, there is a continuing pressure to widen margins on all kinds of consumer lending, keeping interest rates high. Second, banks are busily exploring the profit potential of their retail side for opportunities to increase income from fees and charges (Mitchell 1991).

The result is that there is more explicit pricing of services which consumers previously were led to believe were 'free'. Where consumers were often previously able to maintain a bank account without charge, they may now find themselves faced with explicit pricing of individual banking services, or having to keep a minimum balance in their account to avoid paying charges. Banks' greater sensitivity to costs is leading to the removal of internal cross-subsidisation. The allocation of costs in banking seems to be more of an art than a science, so it may be better to think in terms of changes in the pattern of cross-subsidisation. This move to explicit pricing and higher bank fees and charges – especially onerous on low-income consumers who cannot afford to keep a large minimum balance in their account – is difficult for consumers to resist, although in France the government intervened in 1987 to stop banks charging for cheque transactions.

Improved Consumer Information
In these conditions, and with strong pressures towards increased prices for banking services despite intensified competition, there is an important role that could be played by improved consumer information about bank fees and charges. This has not yet been addressed by the Commission, except in the context of cross-border payments (see the later chapter on this subject). Consumers should have enough accurate

and comprehensible information to enable them to make an effective choice between different banks and different banking services. There is a strong case for information being provided in a standardised form throughout the Community, as a basis for consumers being able to decide where they can best get value for money in banking services. Greater transparency would help to make a single European banking market work more efficiently.

Bank charges are a highly sensitive consumer issue, not least because banks are in the unusual situation of being able to make sure that they get payment by deducting money from consumers' accounts, without the consumer having to take the initiative in making a payment. Sometimes, the consumer is only aware after the event that a charge has been imposed and a payment deducted, when she or he gets a periodic account statement from the bank.

Information about bank charges has become a public policy issue in a number of EC countries. In Denmark, a 1989 study by a consumers' organisation, Forbrugerradet, reached the conclusion that it is not practicable for the consumer to compare the charges levied by different banks, because not enough information is available and because of the different methods of calculation used.

In France, a law passed in 1984 requires banks to notify their charges publicly. The Banque de France (central bank) carried out a study in 1989 to see whether or not banks were complying with their statutory obligation to make their conditions and charges publicly available. In particular, the aim of the study was to find out to what extent banks were using the standardised consumer information notice of charges for seven basic services developed by the banking trade association, the Association Française des Banques (AFB). The study showed that information about charges is available immediately in 95 per cent of the sample of 1,874 bank branches visited, and available on request in a further three per cent. This information is visible from outside the branch premises in less than four per cent of cases, while in 50–60 per cent it is easily visible inside. In 7–10 per cent of branches, information is not easily visible inside or is 'discreet'. More than 28 per cent of branches providing information have no documentation available setting out their general banking conditions. Of those that did have information, in more than one branch in three it is only available on request (Comité Consultatif 1989).

One limitation of the results of this survey is that all banks were notified about it in advance, and each bank branch in the sample was warned that it would be visited by Banque de France inspectors. Two or three weeks earlier, an anonymous survey was carried out by a consumer organisation, Union Fédérale des Consommateurs (UFC), without prior warning. The sample of bank branches was smaller – 400. Of these, 81.5 per cent provide information about charges in the form either of a notice in the window, a notice inside the branch, or leaflets. The remaining branches have no information of any kind. Allowing for the fact that a number of branches only have information available on request, and do not display it, UFC concludes that 45 per cent of the branches it visited are not complying with the spirit of the law (Comité Consultatif 1989).

The pressure in France for consumers to be given advance information about bank charges has been given emphasis by a court ruling (12 April 1988) that a bank should not levy charges on overdrawn customers without telling them in advance what the charges are.

In Spain, the central bank issued an instruction to banks to set out charges and fees in a standardised form as from 1 January 1989. However, it is reported that a consumer organisation, Union de Consumidores de España (UCE) has alleged that there is widespread non-compliance and that much bank information about interest rates payable is misleading (*Retail Banker International* 215, 1990).

The issue of information about bank charges has also been taken up in the UK by the official Review Committee on Banking Services Law and Practice (known as the Jack Committee after the surname of its Chair), which comments that:

> 'Scarcely any topic on which we have consulted has provoked such near unanimity of response. Almost everyone believes that customers should be given more information on the basis used for calculating bank charges, and in some cases feelings appear to run high ... Generally, we should like to see much more transparency imported into the matter of bank charges ... The customer should also be given full details of the method of calculation of fees and charges, when these are applied to his [sic] account ...' (Review Committee on Banking Services Law and Practice 1989)

The Review Committee recommended that banks should explain to their customers the basis of charging for the normal operation of a bank account, including information about any charges that would be imposed if the account was overdrawn. Later evidence on this issue was provided by the results of a national random sample survey of adult UK consumers. 62 per cent of the sample of 1,938 said that they had never been told how bank fees or charges are calculated. Of those who did recall being aware of charges, over half did not know what they would be charged if they overdrew on their accounts (Abbey National 1990).

The Review Committee's recommendation was supported by the UK government in its reponse to the Jack Committee's report, though the emphasis is placed on achieving greater transparency through a code of banking practice rather than through legislation (*Banking Services* – Government Response 1990).

The issue of information about bank charges and interest is indeed dealt with in the draft code of banking practice, issued as a basis for consultation by the UK banks and building societies in December 1990. The draft code requires that:

> 'Banks will provide customers with details of charges, if any, payable in connection with the normal operation of their accounts. This will be in the form of published tariffs. Charges of service outside the tariff will be advised on request or at the time the service is offered. When banks agree to lend money they will tell customers the interest rate payable and when interest will be charged to the account.' *(Draft Code of Banking Practice* 1990)

From the consumer perspective, this is a lame and tame approach to resolving an important issue. There is no indication of the 'core' banking services which should be the subject of published tariffs. There is no attempt – as there is in France – to publish tariff information in a standardised form, so that consumers can compare the tariffs of different banks. There is no indication of how banks should communicate this information, either to their own customers or to consumers more generally. The failure of the UK banks and building societies to deal effectively with the issue of consumer information about charges reinforces the need for the Commission to tackle the question on a Community-wide basis, to give greater transparency to the banking market.

It is surprising that the Commission has not so far taken any initiative on the need for consumers to be given clear and standardised advance information about bank charges, other than in the context of cross-border payments (examined in the relevant chapter, below). It would be a useful way of making the single market for banking services work in practice and there is no obvious reason why it should present the banks with any great difficulties. However, the evidence from France and Spain cited above suggests that any EC measure would need to be effectively monitored to see that it was adhered to by the banks.

Protecting Consumers' Deposits
One issue that has yet to be fully resolved is the need for consumers' deposits to be protected if a bank or other credit institution fails. Many member countries have operated their banking regulatory systems on the basis that no major bank should be allowed to fail. However, changes in regulatory structures and the increasing exposure of banks to market forces mean that the 'too-big-to-fail' syndrome is becoming increasingly outdated. Consumers view with apprehension the disastrous lending experience of many banks to third world countries in the 1970s and to property developers and other corporate borrowers in the mid-1980s. They need assurance that they will not have to pay the price for bad banking practices by losing their deposits if banks crash in the 1990s.

This issue has been brought into sharp focus by the Bank of England's closure in July 1991 of the Luxembourg-registered Bank of Credit and Commerce International (BCCI). Many corporate and individual customers have been badly hit and it is alleged that the worldwide losses may amount to more than $5 billion.

Deposit protection schemes vary widely between member countries – for example, in the maximum covered per bank account and in whether all of the deposit is covered or only a proportion. The Commission first came to grips with this issue in a Recommendation which asked member countries with actual or planned deposit protection schemes to make sure that they met certain criteria. Member countries without schemes were urged to introduce them by 1 January 1990 (European Commission 1986).

The issue has been followed up in the context of the proposed Directive on the winding-up of credit institutions (European Commission 1988a). The ultimate intention is to oblige each member country to ensure that its deposit protection scheme covers not only all banks established in its own territory but also branches which have other EC countries as their home countries – in other words, every branch of an EC bank, wherever established. However, until all member countries have appropriate schemes, those that do will be required to make sure that their schemes cover host country branches of their home country banks. This will mean a degree of harmonisation in deposit guarantee schemes throughout the Community.

In principle, this approach should benefit consumers, though of course much will depend on the detail of the proposals. The Commission's response to the BCCI catastrophe has been that it intends that consumer deposits will be protected in the member country in which the bank concerned does most of its business, rather than the country in which it is registered. It remains to be seen how practical effect will be given to this, especially as some national deposit protection schemes – including the UK scheme – offer only a low level of consumer protection.

The Consumer Agenda

From the consumer viewpoint, the positive side of the Second Banking Directive is that it provides a framework within which Community-wide competition may take place. It may also have the side-effect of intensifying competition in national banking markets in member countries.

The negative side is that there is no guarantee that international competition will be intensified, because of continuing government intervention and because many banks are developing defensive strategies designed to limit the effects of international competition. Also, national consumer protection legislation may be threatened by the central strategy of mutual recognition combined with home country control. The impact should be kept under continual review after the Directive comes into effect. The Commission should also be encouraged to pay attention to the need to improve the transparency of retail banking markets by measures which require consumers to be given clear, standardised, advance information about banking charges and fees. Minimum standards should be set for deposit protection schemes to make sure that consumers' bank deposits are adequately protected throughout the Community.

Borrowing Money

A wide range of different kinds of credit is now available to consumers in EC member countries, including the following:

* Mortgage credit, to help the consumer to buy a house, apartment or land, secured on the property concerned, with fixed or variable interest rates;
* Bank overdraft facilities, open-ended (that is, no fixed term), with a credit ceiling, not linked to any specific purchase;
* Fixed-term personal loans, for a given amount, which may or may not be linked to any specific purchase, but are unsecured, with fixed or variable interest rates;
* Hire purchase, fixed-term, for a given amount, linked to a specific purchase, which may involve the consumer becoming the owner of the product only when payments are completed;
* 'Budget' accounts, open-ended, with a credit ceiling linked to a fixed monthly repayment, not linked to any specific purchase but often limited to purchases at one particular shop or retail group;
* Credit cards, open-ended, with a credit limit, minimum monthly repayment linked to outstanding debt, with or without an annual fee and with variable interest rates: a variant is the charge card (sometimes called travel and entertainment card) where the amount of credit outstanding has to be paid in full at the end of each month.

There has until recently been a clear distinction between mortgage credit and other forms of consumer credit. However, recent years have seen the introduction in some countries, including the UK, of credit which is secured on property but which may be used by the consumer

31

for any purpose she or he chooses – for example, setting up a business, home improvements, consumer durables, holidays, education.

The kinds of financial institutions providing credit are also very varied. They include:

- Banks, including savings and co-operative banks;
- Specialised mortgage lending institutions;
- Finance houses;
- Insurance companies;
- Credit card companies;
- Retailers;
- Government, through the Municipal Credit System (NVVK) in the Netherlands and the Department of Social Security Social Fund in the UK;
- Credit unions.

This pattern of institutional sources of credit is changing in many Community countries, for three reasons:

- Traditional boundaries between the functions of different types of financial institution are breaking down or becoming blurred. For example, in the UK the Building Societies Act 1986 allows specialised mortgage lending institutions, building societies, to offer unsecured personal loans of up to £10,000, while in a number of EC countries the traditional restrictions on the activities of savings banks are being lifted;
- Mergers, takeovers and networking agreements are leading to the emergence of financial conglomerates, some of which are taking on an international character;
- Non-financial institutions such as retailers are entering the field of consumer credit. Examples are Marks and Spencer, House of Fraser, Debenhams and Burtons in the UK, Hertie and Kauphof in Germany and Nouvelles Galeries and Carrefour in France.

This complexity of both *types* and *sources* of credit has considerable implications for the development of policy in relation to credit at Community level. Currently, there are wide differences in legal and regulatory provisions, not only between EC member countries, but within any one country. These controls have tended to be linked to a particular type or source of credit, but there is little consistency from country to country.

The Growth in Consumer Indebtedness

New types of consumer credit and new institutional sources have contributed to a rapid expansion in consumer indebtedness in many EC countries. For example, the figures in the UK are as follows:

Consumer debt outstanding in UK at end-year (£million)

	Housing debt	Personal debt	All consumer debt
1984	108,535	22,307	130,842
1985	127,568	26,112	153,680
1986	154,183	30,212	184,395
1987	183,363	36,270	220,633
1988	222,189	42,707	264,896
1989	255,823	48,709	304,532

(*Financial Statistics* February 1991)

These figures show that, in money terms, total consumer indebtedness more than doubled in the five years to end-1989, with housing debt (that is, mortgages) rising slightly faster than personal debt. Taking price increases into account, both forms of debt have more than doubled *in real terms* since 1980.

What do these national figures mean for individual households? The average total indebtedness per UK household was £14,365 at end-1989, of which £12,067 was housing debt and £2,298 personal debt. However, these figures do not take account of the fact that, at any one time, only 37% of UK households have a mortgage (General Household Survey 1985), while an estimated 47% have some personal debt outstanding (Office of Fair Trading 1988). Taking these proportions into account, at end-1989 those households with mortgages had an outstanding housing debt which averaged £32,614. Those households with any personal debt averaged £4,889 outstanding.

These are very considerable sums, certainly compared with previous periods. They represent a substantial increase in the ratio of household debt to income, though it is only fair to point out that the ratio of debt to assets has not changed greatly. This is largely because of the rise in the absolute and real value of house prices that has taken place in the UK over the last 20 years (despite the recent downturn).

How does the use of credit and the level of indebtedness vary among different kinds of UK households? Age is a significant factor. Of those between 25 and 44 years old, 89% use one or more types of credit, including mortgages. The proportion falls to 73% among people between 45 and 64 and is as low as 28% among the elderly (over 65 years old). Among young adults between 18 and 24 years old, 71% are credit users. Households with children are more likely to use credit than those without (Office of Fair Trading 1988: Jubilee Centre 1988: Berthoud 1990).

Evidence about how the amount of indebtedness is related to income in UK households is less easy to interpret. Use of credit and the amount of indebtedness both increase with income. At any given level of income, households with children are more likely to use credit and to owe more than those without children. Low income households with children appear to be a particularly vulnerable group (Berthoud 1990).

Overindebtedness

International comparisons are difficult to make, because the statistics are not standardised. However, 'overindebtedness' is looked on as a major public policy issue in a number of EC countries, including Germany and the Netherlands. In France, the official banking Comité Consultatif, on which consumers are represented, was asked to examine and comment on the Government's draft legislation on Prevention and Control of Difficulties Linked to the Overindebtedness of Individuals and Families (Law no.89.1010 of 31 December 1989). In the UK, a survey commissioned by the Office of Fair Trading points to some 11 per cent of all households (2.3 million) having experienced difficulties in keeping up loan repayments at some time during the previous five years (Office of Fair Trading 1988). The National Consumer Council has expressed anxiety at the increase in the number of consumers (estimated at one million) with loans secured on their houses for a wide variety of other purposes including buying cars and setting up businesses, which could make their homes vulnerable to repossession if they fail to maintain their repayments (National Consumer Council 1987). At Community level, it is understood that work has now been resumed within the Commission on the preparation of a draft Convention on insolvency procedures.

However, it would be a mistake for consumer representatives to look on credit *per se* as undesirable. It is a way in which people can obtain things they need or want but cannot immediately afford. The long-standing moral disapproval of credit has wilted as a result of a major change in consumer attitudes. Traditional proverbs about credit and debt – 'Neither a borrower nor a lender be', 'Out of debt, out of danger' – have rapidly acquired a musty, antiquarian flavour which seems to many people to be of little relevance to modern life. Any moral stigma attached to indebtedness is disappearing in all age groups and all countries, and at all levels of income. Using credit is now an integral and largely unavoidable part of the fabric of life – '… a socially acceptable form of financial transaction' (Ford 1988).

Within the context of this growing use of credit by consumers, and the problems of overindebtedness which affect a minority, what are the main consumer policy issues? They focus on:

- The advertising and marketing techniques used to sell credit;
- Consumer information about the cost of credit;
- The terms and conditions on which credit is provided;
- The help that should be available for the 'credit casualties' who find that they are unable to manage their overindebtedness.

Advertising and Marketing Credit

A sea-change has taken place in the relationships between consumers and financial institutions. Consumers are increasingly willing to use credit as a normal part of their household financial management, while financial institutions have come to realise that consumer credit is a highly profitable and relatively secure form of business.

This change is evident in the introduction of sophisticated ways of advertising and marketing credit to consumers. In many EC countries (though there are exceptions, such as Germany), credit is marketed as a financial service in its own right, outside any pre-existing relationship between bank and customer. Many consumers now have a variety of different kinds of credit from a range of different financial institutions. Press and television advertising are complemented by direct mail, both to existing customers and to lists of names and addresses which are bought on the basis of their likely suitability as credit customers.

An extreme example was the initial launch of credit cards in the UK by an unsolicited mailing to many consumers, who found themselves in possession of a credit card whether they wanted one or not. The public and Parliamentary protest that followed led to a prohibition on this being included in the Consumer Credit Act 1974 (there is a similar provision in the Danish Payment Cards Act 1984). However, the consumer may be offered an incentive to take out a loan or apply for a credit card – examples include a travel bag, a road atlas and a luxury ballpoint pen. Once the consumer has a credit card, she or he may be offered a further incentive – for example, a case of wine – to suggest the names and addresses of other consumers who might apply.

The UK also has a record of schemes designed to persuade cardholders to spend more money using their credit cards, and so increase their indebtedness. For example, if the holder of a Co-operative Bank Visa card used the card to spend £500 in a limited period, she or he got a 35mm. camera, with lower value rewards if less than £500 was spent. Barclaycard had a scheme called 'Profiles', in which the consumer scored one point for every £10 of purchases during a calendar year. The consumer could then choose so-called 'gifts' from a catalogue – at the top end of the scale, anyone who spent £75,000 in one calendar year using a Barclaycard was entitled to a 'gift' of a stereo sound system. National Westminster Bank Access credit card participated in the Air Miles promotion scheme – the consumer was credited with one free air mile for every £10 spent (Mitchell 1989).

Another practice has been for card issuers to increase the limit on a credit card without being asked to by the consumer. It has been a common experience among UK cardholders, at least among those who repay regularly, to have their credit limit increased as they approach or exceed the existing limit. However, prohibition of this practice is among a series of proposals recently put forward by the UK Government to tighten up controls on credit marketing (Department of Trade and Industry 1990b).

The UK has a wide-ranging set of controls which govern the form and content of both advertisements and written information to consumers. For example, when credit would be secured on a consumer's home, the advertisement must carry a 'health' warning that the home is at risk if the consumer fails to keep up repayments. An advertisement for credit (for example, a mortgage) in a foreign currency must warn that the cost could be affected by exchange rate movements. There are also strict boundaries to the way words such as 'overdraft', 'no deposit' and 'interest free' may be used (*Advertisements and Quotations Regulations* 1989).

As has been mentioned, the UK Government is proposing to strengthen these controls over credit marketing and advertising. For example, all credit advertisements will have to include the statement 'Warning – do not enter into a credit agreement unless you are sure that you can afford the payments'. An advertisement for credit which is subject to a variable rate of interest will have to include the statement – 'Warning – charges may be increased after the agreement is made'. There are various other provisions intended to make consumers more aware, through advertising for credit, of the responsibilities and hazards of using credit (Department of Trade and Industry 1990b).

In France, statutory controls over the advertising and marketing of credit have recently been supplemented by a self-regulatory 'ethical code', under the aegis of the advertising control body, the Bureau de Verification de la Publicité. The principle underlying this code is that the importance to the consumer of taking on credit commitments should not be minimised in advertising. In particular, it should be made clear just what offers of 'free' or subsidised credit, or delayed repayments, involve (*Les Notes Bleues*, 28 May 1990).

The Cost of Credit

The governments of many EC member countries now impose controls on the ways in which the cost of credit is advertised to consumers. For example, Denmark, France, Germany, the Netherlands and the UK have regulations which require that, if information about credit terms or the cost of credit is given in advertisements, then the cost of credit must be stated in a prescribed manner. The principles underlying this are:

*   The total costs of credit to the consumer should include not only interest but also any other charges which the consumer has to pay for the credit;
*   These costs should be expressed as an Annual Percentage Rate of charge (APR) which takes account of repayments made during the course of the loan.

There are at present, however, variations between countries in the details of the way in which these principles are applied in Community countries – this issue is examined under Commission Initiatives later.

As well as advertising controls, regulations in Denmark and France require banks to display information about the costs of credit in their branches, though compliance with and the effectiveness of these regulations have been the subject of criticism by consumer organisations in both countries. The Government also takes a hand in France in making sure that the cost of credit is in the public domain: at the beginning of each quarter the Minister of Economy, Finance and the Budget publishes the credit interest rates applied by credit institutions during the preceding three months to personal loans, consumer credit and mortgages. For example, one set of figures shows interest rates for personal loans varying from 14.10 per cent to 17.96 per cent and for consumer credit from 14.40 per cent to 17.96 per cent. Interest rates are also given for varying types of mortgages. Ranges are given, but not figures for individual financial institutions (*Journal Officiel* 5 July 1989).

For those committed to the consumer principles of value for money and the use of comparative information to obtain it, empirical research on UK consumers' knowledge and use of interest rates produces gloomy results. An Office of Fair Trading Survey indicates that over half of current or recent UK credit users do not know what APR (Annual Percentage Rate of charge) means, against roughly a quarter who do. Among non-users of credit – who are, after all, potential users – less than one in 10 understand the concept of APR. Knowledge and understanding are particularly low among both women and those in the lower occupational groups.

Once the true meaning of APR is explained to survey respondents, just under half of current and recent credit users say that they have ever referred to APR when making credit arrangements. Within this group, only 45 per cent are able to make a reasonably realistic estimate of the current APR on credit card debt. Even this is higher than the proportion – about 25 per cent – who can make an approximate estimate of the cost of a bank loan (Office of Fair Trading 1989).

These depressing results confirm the general picture of previous survey results, not only from the UK but also from the US, about the slow progress being made in improving consumers' use of disclosed APR figures for different sources of credit as a way of obtaining value for money. They tend to justify the view – widespread in the financial services industry – that consumer demand for credit is insensitive to interest rates. One outcome is that the UK Government is proposing that if the APR is stated in a credit advertisement it should be supplemented by information about the actual monetary cost of credit, in order to bring home to consumers what taking out a loan involves (Department of Trade and Industry 1990b).

In a number of Community countries, requirements to disclose the cost of credit are set within a framework of controls on the maximum interest rate that can be charged. This approach is not a new one – it stems from historic prohibitions of usury. In Belgium and the Netherlands, interest rate ceilings are fixed according to the size, duration and type of loan, linked by formulae to prevailing interest rate levels in the money market. A conscious decision has recently been taken in the Netherlands to renew the system of interest rate ceilings, on the grounds that it is a valuable instrument in limiting consumer overindebtedness and as such is preferable to the largely unused UK system of giving the courts power to reopen 'extortionate' credit agreements. A similar system has also recently been renewed in France, but with changed formulae, in Law no.89.1010 of 31 December 1989, following advice given by the Comité Consultatif (Comité Consultatif 1989: Kessler 1988).

Terms and Conditions

Credit agreements frequently take the form of standard form contracts subject to differing degrees and forms of statutory control, which vary between and often within member countries. Variation within any one country may depend on the type and source of credit. For example, regulations about credit card contracts may be very different from those about bank overdrafts. Statutory controls may be negative in form, that is prohibiting certain types of contractual clauses, or they may be positive, requiring certain provisions to be included. Both forms have the same objectives of redressing the inequitable balance of bargaining power between the individual consumer and the financial institution and of limiting the consumer's vulnerability when standard form contracts are used as the basis of making credit available.

In Germany, standard terms and conditions of credit agreements must be drawn to the consumer's attention or displayed clearly in the place where the agreement is concluded (Contract Conditions Act). Under new proposed legislation, the consumer must be given a draft written loan agreement and has the right to cancel within one week. In France, the financial institution granting credit must make a preliminary offer, setting out the rate of interest and other conditions, which remains open to the consumer to accept or reject for a period of 15 days. The conditions of the offer cannot be changed during that time. Following the consumer's acceptance, there is a further cooling-off period, which is normally seven days (Law no.78.22 of 10 January 1978). These periods of delay are built into the legal procedures to give the consumer the opportunity of examining and considering the terms of the credit contract without being under pressure to sign immediately.

In the UK, information disclosure provisions for regulated credit agreements provide for the consumer to have a clear written record of the terms of the agreement and her or his rights under it. This includes information about the consumer's right to complete payments ahead of time and the right to receive a rebate of a proportion of the total credit charges when doing so (Consumer Credit Act 1974).

In some countries, statutory disclosure requirements about the terms and conditions of a credit agreement are supplemented by disclosure requirements laid down in industry self-regulatory codes of practice. In the UK, the Finance Houses Association Code of Practice requires its member institutions to ensure that the consumer is made aware, where appropriate, of the availability of credit protection insurance. It also sets out internal company review procedures to be followed where a consumer is refused credit and believes the refusal to be unreasonable. Members undertake to use plain language in all communications with the consumer and in particular to provide clear statements of terms and conditions (Finance Houses Association 1987). The Retail Credit Group, which represents leading UK retailers in their capacity as credit granters and issuers of credit cards, also follows this Code of Practice.

In the Netherlands, a self-regulatory Mortgage Loans Code of Conduct came into effect in 1990. This requires member institutions to state the effective rate of interest in all offers. It also includes a provision that a mortgage contract cannot subsequently be varied in any way which harms the consumer's interest. In France, the banking trade organisation, Association Française des Banques, has recently introduced a code of conduct in relation to the lending practices of banks. This includes the introduction by each bank of an appeals procedure for consumers who are initially refused credit (*Actualité Bancaire* 19 February 1990).

Help for Credit Casualties

What is a credit casualty? At what stage does indebtedness become *over*indebtedness? How many consumers are credit casualties and what can be done to help them? In the UK, it is clear from a variety of sources that the majority of consumers do not consider their indebtedness a burden, but that for a minority it represents a problem. For example, a national sample survey concludes that:

> 'Most credit users felt happy with their present commitments and, indeed, many felt that they could take on more. Few users expressed worries about paying off their debts in future, although there were some instances of considerable credit repayment difficulties among a minority of the sample.' (Office of Fair Trading 1988)

It is not easy to quantify either the proportion of consumers who may be accurately described as the casualties of credit, or the extent of their problem. However, the same survey provides a crude measure of the former, and focuses on the contributory factors:

> 'Just over a tenth of credit users had experienced difficulties with repayment in the last five years, the greatest incidence being among

the 18-24 age group, and those who were divorced or separated. Over a third of those who had experienced difficulties had stopped payments for a time. Respondents had most frequently experienced problems with meeting payments on credit cards, with mortgages second most difficult. The major contributory factors leading to problems were a sudden loss of earnings or a mismanagement of funds, either through taking on too many credit commitments, or overspending on a particular item.' (OFT 1988)

This survey report goes on to itemise the main reasons for loss of earnings as redundancy, job loss, strike and loss of overtime. Other sources, especially money advisers who are in direct contact with consumers with serious financial problems, confirm marital or relationship breakdown and loss of earnings as the main reasons why people find it difficult to repay their debts (Andrews 1988). The most serious debt problems are found amongst unemployed families with children – more than half of them are in arrears with repayments (Berthoud 1990). A detailed analysis of the incomes and expenditures of credit casualties shows that a number of households with very low or irregular incomes never had any realistic chance of paying off the debts they had incurred. (Jubilee Centre 1988). There are indicators which suggest that the number of credit casualties is increasing, for example in the rise in mortgage arrears and repossessions, but it is not, however, possible to make even an informed guess about the rate of increase in credit casualties.

One factor that needs to be taken into account in considering support services is that credit casualties are increasingly committed to debts to many different credit suppliers. A survey of over 1,000 UK credit casualties shows that 48 per cent have between three and six separate debts, and that a further 38 per cent have seven or more debts. One respondent had as many as 30 debts. The significance of new sources of credit is apparent from the fact that one third of credit casualties are in debt to credit card issuers, often for relatively large amounts (Jubilee Trust 1988). It is clear that support services should be provided which help the consumer who is a credit casualty to make a comprehensive plan to deal with all her or his debts.

International comparisons are difficult because of the lack of remotely comparable figures. However, in the Netherlands around 3.4 per cent of households are reported to be overindebted, while in France the figure in absolute terms is said to be 200,000 (*Unemployment and Consumer Debts in Europe* 1989).

The provision of non-profit money advice (debt counselling) services is growing in a number of countries. In the Netherlands, the Consumer and Household Foundation, a Government-subsidised organisation, trains money advisers who are paid by local councils. In Germany there is a loosely structured money advice network provided by consumer organisations and local councils. The Citizens' Advice Bureaux in the UK are placing increasing emphasis on money advice, while there are also some independent money advice centres, with the the involvement of some local councils. In other Community countries, such as Spain and Greece, there is little in the way of money advice beyond the traditional functions of some private charities.

Increasingly, money advice services go beyond giving advice to arranging the rescheduling of debts with creditors or, in the Netherlands, the refinancing of debts through the municipal credit banks – the NVVK. However, there is plenty of evidence that the supply of such services throughout the EC hardly begins to meet the demand and there is a shortage of resources to run them (Andrews 1988: Hinton and Berthoud 1988).

Another practical problem is how consumers who are in trouble over debt repayments can get to know what services are available to help them. In the UK, a telephone 'Helpline' was run in conjunction with a BBC week-long radio campaign on managing credit and dealing with debt. The Helpline not only gave information and advice to callers, but referred them where appropriate to a debt counselling service. 35 per cent of the 5,672 callers had debt problems, and of these, no less than 95 per cent had not sought any previous help. This is an indication of the information gap about debt counselling services (Broadcasting Support Services 1989).

The gap has been partly filled by a telephone 'National Debtline' over which two or three staff handle calls at the rate of 5,000 a year. A survey of callers shows that 63 per cent had paid off their arrears or were paying them off satisfactorily, while 60 per cent said they were budgeting better as a result of the help they had received (Stanton 1991).

Mortgage Credit
The variations between Community countries in the channels of supply of mortgage credit and its regulatory control are even greater than they are for other forms of consumer credit. A number of countries have specialised lending institutions, though these rarely have a monopoly of mortgage credit and may be competing with commercial banks and, in some cases, insurance companies. In the UK and Ireland, there are

Building Societies. Italy has Credito Fondiario, either as self-contained departments of banks or as separate institutions. Spain has Sociedades de Credito Hipotecario as well as Cajas de Ahorro (savings banks). In Germany there are Mortgage Banks and Bausparkassen.

The strong public policy interest in making sure that there is an adequate supply of housing available at reasonable cost is recognised in many countries by an elaborate framework of regulation. For example, there are frequently controls over the maximum amount of a mortgage in relation to the value of the house or flat being bought – 80 per cent in Denmark and Spain, 50 per cent in France and 60 per cent in Germany unless any additional percentage is covered by a public institution's guarantee. In Denmark and Germany, only the value of the property may be taken into account in determining the maximum size of the mortgage, not the consumer's income or personal financial standing. There are notable differences in whether interest rates are fixed or variable during the period of the mortgage – and if variable, the intervals and limits of variation.

Public policy interest extends to arrangements for the funding of mortgages, with varying patterns of funding by bond issues and by consumer deposits. Mortgages linked to life insurance policies are unknown in Denmark but common in the UK. State-owned institutions are involved in wholesale (and sometimes retail) funding arrangements in some countries – for example, the Office Central de Crédit Hypothecaire in Belgium and the Banco Hipotecario in Spain. There are also major differences in the treatment of taxation (European Community Mortgage Federation 1990).

To add to the Community kaleidoscope on mortgage credit, the consumer protection and information provisions within any one country may be partly the same for mortgage credit and for other forms of consumer credit – or may be altogether different.

Continuing Chaos or Emerging Order?
This chapter is able only to outline the striking differences in approaches to both institutional structures for making credit available and the legal frameworks for credit regulation, not only between EC member countries, but within any one country. These are most marked in relation to mortgage credit but are in fact pervasive throughout all kinds of consumer credit. The variations are the outcome of a number of different strands of public policy, which are often mutually conflicting, including the following:

- Regulation of the quantity and nature of credit has been seen as one of the cornerstones of macro-economic control, though this is weakening as a result of the liberalisation of capital movements between countries and domestic deregulation;
- Specific regulatory regimes have tended to be associated with particular types of credit – for example, mortgage credit or hire purchase and instalment credit. There have tended to be regulatory inconsistencies as between one kind of credit and another. Newer forms of credit – for example, credit cards and revolving credit – are less likely to be regulated;
- Consumer protection and information strategy tends to be a varying mixture of three separate elements – improving market transparency so that consumers can make optimal choices, preventing the abuse of market power by credit granters and the prevention or remedying of overindebtedness.

Nevertheless, in spite of this diversity, a degree of policy consensus is emerging throughout EC countries, focusing primarily on information disclosure requirements aimed at improved market transparency. These elements of consensus include the following:

- In any advertising and marketing of credit, if the cost of credit is mentioned it should be expressed in terms of the APR, so that the consumer can compare the cost of credit from different sources;
- Before a loan agreement is concluded, the consumer should be told the APR, and how this is determined if it is variable either continuously or periodically during the course of the loan;
- The consumer should be told all charges, fees and commission to be paid as a result of taking out a loan and these should be included in the APR calculation;
- The consumer should not be put under any pressure to take out a loan and should (in either some or all circumstances) be given time to decide either not to proceed with or to cancel the loan;
- All loan agreements should be in writing and their terms and conditions should be fair;
- Credit granters should be under a formal or informal obligation to engage in 'responsible lending', for example by always consulting a credit reference agency and by taking into account the consumer's ability to repay a loan;
- Consumers should have the right to repay their loans early, on a pro rata basis.

- The regulatory controls and information disclosure provisions for different types of credit should converge, with variations only where necessary (for example, with mortgage credit).
- Improved consumer information may help to prevent over-indebtedness, but other public policy initiatives (for example, subsidised money advice services) may be necessary to help consumers who get into difficulties, usually through no fault of their own.

Commission Initiatives

The Commission's work on consumer credit (other than mortgage credit) started in 1979, along the lines of the 'old approach', involving detailed harmonisation. The First Consumer Credit Directive (87/102/EEC) was eventually adopted on 22 December 1986, with an implementation date of 1 January 1990. The key provisions of the Directive do not cover mortgage credit and are diluted for bank overdrafts. Credit agreements for amounts less than 200 ECU and more than 20,000 ECU are excluded from its scope.

The content of the Directive was weakened at a late stage of negotiations, following national and international lobbying by the financial services industry and opposition to many of the harmonisation provisions by the governments of several member countries, including the UK. Provisions that disappeared from the proposed Directive before it was adopted included connected lender liability (comparable with section 75 of the UK Consumer Credit Act 1974), obligatory licensing of credit granting institutions, and protection of consumers from unfair credit contract clauses. These key consumer protection issues were left to be dealt with by national legislation and this First Consumer Credit Directive has been strongly criticised by BEUC for its inadequacy.

The Directive's most important provisions are about information on the cost of credit. If an advertisement for credit includes a rate of interest or any figures about the cost of credit, then it must also include the APR. All credit agreements must be in writing and should include both the APR and, for agreements where the APR may change during the course of the loan, a statement of the conditions under which the APR may be changed. However, 'where it is not possible' to state the APR, the consumer should be told the annual rate of interest – that is, the 'flat' rate of interest which does not take account of repayments made during the course of the loan – and any charges. This first fallback provision involving the use of a flat rate of interest also applies to bank overdrafts.

There is a second fallback position which allows member countries which do not have an established method of calculating APR to require only the total cost of credit to be indicated. The decision on a common, Community-wide method of calculating the APR is deferred and it is left to member countries to continue to use their existing rules either for calculating the APR or for otherwise indicating the cost of credit.

An important consumer protection requirement (not previously available, for example, in Germany) incorporated in the Directive is that consumers should be entitled to repay fixed term credit agreements before the due date with '... an equitable reduction in the total cost of credit'. Written credit agreements should include essential terms of the contract and illustrative lists of these for different forms of credit are given in an Annex.

The draft provisions about licensing appear in very diluted form in the final text. Governments of member countries are required *either* to ensure that there is official licensing of credit granting financial institutions *or* to ensure that such institutions are officially inspected *or* to promote the setting up of bodies to handle consumer complaints and provide consumer information.

However, the main consumer criticism of the First Consumer Credit Directive must be that it scarcely begins to tackle the obstacles to a single market in consumer credit that stem from wide differences from country to country in the legal structures governing credit, especially so far as consumer protection is concerned. The provisions about information disclosure of the costs of credit are also inadequate, in that they allow the continuance of the use of the misleading 'flat' rate of interest as well as not providing any common method of calculating APR.

This last point – but not the more general weaknesses – has been tackled in the Second Consumer Credit Directive (90/88/EEC) of 22 February 1990, which has an implementation date of 31 December 1992. Its main function is to establish a Community-wide method of calculating the APR by specifying the mathematical formula that should be used. In principle, this is an improvement because it makes it possible for the consumer to compare the relative cost of different sources of credit both within and between member countries. However, it will be some time before this principle comes fully into practice. Any member country which, on 1 March 1990, uses a different formula for calculating the APR may continue using it for up to three years *after* the date of implementation – that is, up to 31 December 1995. The two countries concerned, which put up a strong fight against having to change their formulae, are France and Germany (France uses the 'nominal' actuarial method and Germany the '360-day' method).

Following protracted discussions, this Second Credit Directive specifies that all types of credit charges should be included in the total cost of credit, and hence in the APR calculation, other than those specifically listed. However, it is a weakness that the exception allowing the 'flat' rate of interest to continue to be used in relation to overdrafts persists in this Second Directive. Moreover, the exemption in relation to mortgage credit is now extended to all forms of credit secured on property, whether or not the credit is used for home purchase or improvement.

Proposals for a Directive on mortgage credit were launched in 1984 and amended in 1987. However, much of the substance of what the Commission had in mind was incorporated in the wider-ranging proposals for the Second Banking Directive (89/646/EEC) of 15 December 1989. A subsequent revised, informal and unpublished draft on mortgage credit dealt with the mutual recognition of what are called 'financial techniques', including methods for funding loans (for example, direct deposits from the public, bond issues and wholesale funding) and the contractual elements of granting mortgage loans (for example, size and duration of loan, fixed or variable interest, APR and frequency of payment).

Progress on a separate mortgage credit Directive appears to have come to a standstill at the time of writing, because of the wide differences between EC member countries in relation to the laws of property, taxation and the regulatory structure for mortgage lending. There may be scope for a limited initiative developing a common methodology for expressing the APR for mortgage credit and establishing the consumer's right to repay a mortgage early. These would parallel what has been done for personal credit in the Second Consumer Credit Directive. The prospects for any further work which is specific to mortgage credit do not at present look good.

The Consumer Agenda

A genuinely Community-wide market for credit would undoubtedly benefit consumers. There are at present wide differences between EC countries in the interest rates for both mortgage and personal credit and the higher interest rates would come under strong pressure if consumers had the freedom in practice to obtain credit wherever it was cheapest.

Other current developments within the EC should also in principle provide more favourable conditions for a single market in credit – for example, the strengthening of the ERM and the eventual possibility of a single currency should reduce or eliminate the exchange rate risks of cross-border credit.

However, the First and Second Consumer Credit Directives and the Second Banking Directive have not put in place the minimum harmonisation of consumer protection provisions which is a necessary condition for a truly effective single market in credit. They have not really begun to tackle the wide differences in legal provisions and regulatory structures which continue to be a barrier. In spite of the formidable obstacles these differences present, there are three issues which are relatively self-contained and on which initiatives by the Commission might accelerate the development of a single market in credit. These are credit reference systems, action on default and discrimination.

Credit Reference Systems
Whether or not a consumer gets an offer of credit is becoming increasingly dependent on the credit supplier's use of a credit reference agency. At present, there are big differences in the way that credit reference systems work. In the Netherlands, credit suppliers are obliged to take responsible decisions: this implies, amongst other things, checking a credit applicant with the central credit reporting agency, the Stichting Bureau Kredietregistratie. In Denmark, private credit reference agencies are controlled by the Private Registers Act 1978 (amended 1988). Credit reference agencies operate at länder level in Germany, grouped together nationally in the Protective Association for General Credit Precautions (SCHUFA). In France, there is a national credit register under the aegis of the Banque de France (central bank), but the law provides that only serious cases of delayed or non-payment should be recorded. In the UK, private credit reference agencies have to be licensed under the Consumer Credit Act. There is considerable controversy about the kinds of data that they store and what kinds of data credit suppliers should be allowed to retrieve in relation to individual credit grant applications. Indeed, enforcement notices served by the Data Protection Registrar on the four main credit reference agencies requiring them to change their credit reference computer systems are currently the subject of appeal before the Data Protection Tribunal.

All these systems are *nationally* based and all operate within different legal and regulatory structures. Their distinct national bases constitute an obstacle to the development of a single credit market, because it is either impossible or extremely difficult for a supplier of credit in country A to obtain a credit reference about a consumer who lives in country B. The Commission should explore what minimum conditions are needed to allow for the networking of credit reference agencies, taking full account of the privacy factors outlined in the chapter on Protecting Personal Financial Information.

Action on Default

There are major differences between EC member countries in the courses of action open to a credit supplier if the consumer falls behind with payments or defaults. These include the imposition of financial penalties by the credit supplier, anatocism (charging interest on interest), charging the costs of debt recovery, wage assignment or garnishing, refinancing at higher rates of interest, and the bankruptcy of the consumer. Credit suppliers are reluctant to lend to residents of other countries because of uncertainty about the procedures that may be used if the consumer defaults – even about which country's laws apply. The same uncertainties apply to the consumer. The Commission should examine what can be done to put sanctions and procedures in the event of default on a common basis.

Discrimination

There seems a very real possibility that financial institutions will negate the objective of a single market for credit by discriminating against nationals of or residents in other EC countries. There is evidence for this in a comparative cross-frontier study carried out in Belgium and North-Eastern France. Nine of 13 credit supplying financial institutions in North-Eastern France said they would not consider granting credit to a non-resident Belgian, while no less than 26 out of the 27 Belgian institutions surveyed would not lend to a non-resident French national (*Le Crédit à la Consommation* 1988). If these policies are widespread, they will be a major obstacle to the development of a single market for credit. However, they are part of a more general problem of discrimination dealt with in the final chapter.

Payment Cards

The last decade has seen dramatic growth in the availability of plastic cards that can be used by consumers for a wide range of different payment purposes, including the following:

- Withdrawing cash from an Automated Teller Machine (ATM);
- Making deposits in an ATM;
- Asking for a new cheque book or a bank statement via an ATM;
- Paying for goods and services with a cheque accompanied by a cheque guarantee card, by which the bank guarantees the retailer the value of the cheque up to a fixed ceiling;
- Paying for goods and services with a credit card linked to an account which provides extended credit to the consumer;
- Paying for goods and services with a charge card (sometimes called a travel and entertainment card) linked to an account which is settled on a monthly basis;
- Paying for goods and services with a debit card which triggers electronic payment from the consumer's account to the retailer's account.

Any one card may combine one, two or more of these payment functions. For example, one card may be both a cheque guarantee card and a credit card. Some payment systems are still paper-based, taking an imprint from the consumer's card on to a paper voucher. There is a widening use of electronic systems, in which the consumer's card is used in a terminal in conjunction with an 'identifier' such as a signature or Personal Identification Number (PIN). One such system is Electronic Funds Transfer at Point of Sale (EFTPOS), in which the consumer can use a credit, charge or debit card to pay for goods and services, dispensing with cash and cheque payments.

The range of commercial organisations issuing cards is widening. It includes banks, building societies, other financial institutions such as American Express and Diners Club, and retailers. Increasingly, any one card issuing organisation may offer a variety of different kinds of card.

While the use of payment cards by consumers is increasing everywhere in the EC, there are wide variations from country to country. For example, as the table below shows, the density of ATMs per million inhabitants varies from 339 in Spain down to 15 in Greece.

Density of ATMs per million inhabitants in EC countries (January 1990)

Spain	339
UK	282
France	234
Denmark	156
Netherlands	133
Belgium	126
Ireland	123
Germany	114
Italy	108
Luxembourg	106
Portugal	71
Greece	15
Japan	650
USA	327

(*Source*: Battelle Institute 1990)

After a lengthy period of hesitant experiment, EFTPOS systems are now beginning to take root. There are probably now some 250,000–300,000 retail EFTPOS terminals in the EC (personal estimate), with France, Spain, the UK, Belgium and Denmark in the forefront of development. In 1989, EFTPOS accounted for 8 per cent of non-cash payments in Belgium, 7 per cent in France and 6 per cent in the UK (Battelle Institute 1991).

It would be wrong to assume that new developments in payment systems are necessarily linked to high levels of economic prosperity. For example, Germany is towards the bottom of the list of EC countries in terms of both the density of ATMs and EFTPOS development. There are significant differences between countries both in the customary ways that consumers pay for goods and services and in the views taken by banks and other financial institutions about investment priorities and about the needs of their customers. Nevertheless, technological developments in payment systems – which know no frontiers – are likely to lead to a long-term convergence in consumers' approach to payments.

The Consumer Balance Sheet

The plastic card revolution has brought benefits to many consumers. Using a cheque guarantee card gives the retailer the assurance of a bank guarantee of payment and reduces the uncertainty or embarrassment of a cheque being refused. It is now easier for us to get at our money by withdrawing cash from ATMs, especially during the evenings and at weekends, when banks are closed. The specific advantages of EFTPOS are less clear, but market research by banks shows that some consumers find it more convenient than paying by cash or cheque. There is now a much wider choice of payment methods open to consumers than there was 20 – or even 10 – years ago.

There are, however, some problems. While the great majority of card transactions go through without difficulty, a small minority cause considerable trouble. For example, in the UK complaints about disputed card transactions constitute the largest single category of complaints received by both the Banking Ombudsman and the Building Societies' Ombudsman (Banking Ombudsman 1990; Building Societies' Ombudsman 1990). Card problems have been a focus of attention for consumer organisations in a number of EC countries, including Belgium, Denmark, France, Germany, the Netherlands and Spain (see for example National Consumer Council 1985) and have been taken up at EC level by BEUC and European Consumer Law Group (Bourgoignie and Goyens 1990).

The problems encountered by consumers include the following:

- Consumers may be sent payment cards and/or PINs although they have not asked for them;
- Consumers may not be given enough information about their rights and responsibilities when using cards;
- There may be a lack of clarity about the precise moment at which a payment card contract comes into force;
- Consumers may not be given a printed record of a payment card transaction;
- Payment card contracts are drawn up unilaterally by the card issuer;
- Card issuers make unilateral changes to the terms of the contract and often without giving consumers adequate notification of the changes;

- Contracts may be written in obscure legal language;
- Consumers are frequently held liable for the unauthorised use of payment cards when they have been lost or stolen, sometimes after the loss or theft has been notified to the card issuer. Their accounts are debited with transactions carried out by others without their knowledge or authorisation;
- Some card issuers do not provide adequate round-the-clock facilities to enable consumers to report the loss or theft of cards;
- When a consumer disputes whether a transaction has taken place or whether it was authorised, she or he is often faced with an impossible burden of proof;
- Card issuers often disclaim liability for consumer losses caused by faults in their systems or equipment;
- In many EC member countries, there are no cheap, rapid and effective procedures for resolving disputes between the consumer and the card issuing organisation.

This long catalogue of consumer problems with cards would not matter so much if there was effective consumer protection legislation which dealt specifically with payment cards, but, with the sole exception of Denmark, this is not the case. In other EC countries, some aspects of payment card usage are caught accidentally by legislation designed primarily for other purposes. Otherwise, consumers' use of payment cards is governed by the contracts drawn up by card issuers. Only in the Netherlands are these negotiated between the consumer organisation and the banks – elsewhere they are issued unilaterally and are invariably one-sided. The unfairness to the consumer of the great majority of these contracts has been fully documented in other publications and there is no need to repeat it here (Mitchell 1988a, 1988b: European Consumer Law Group 1989: Allix 1990: Bourgoignie and Goyens 1990).

However, if there is one key issue on which consumer protection should be focused, it is that many cards combine a one-sided contract with a vulnerable user-identification technology, the PIN. If a payment card is used in conjunction with its associated PIN, the contract makes the assumption that the transaction is authorised. This means that if the card and PIN are both lost or stolen together, the consumer is financially at risk until the loss or theft is noticed and reported to the card issuer. Consumer organisations within the EC have worked hard during the last few years to put this and other payment card consumer protection issues high on the public policy agenda. The extent to which they have succeeded in doing this and the issues that remain outstanding are examined in the rest of this chapter.

The European Commission's Strategy

The Commission's strategy for new payment methods is set out in *Europe Could Play an Ace: the New Payment Cards* (1987a). The principal goal is 'interoperability' for card-based payment systems, defined as consumers being able to use payment cards issued in one EC country to withdraw cash from ATMs and buy goods and services in other EC countries, irrespective of the technology used. Interoperability of payment cards is seen by the Commission as an essential element in the single market for financial services.

The Commission's strategy also has a strong secondary goal linked to the EC's industrial policy. A large and stable EC-wide market for card-based payment systems would help to develop a cohesive electronic payments industry, bringing together hardware manufacturers, software suppliers and card issuers. This industry would be able to compete in world markets with the US and Japan and 'could open up huge external markets for the Community, enabling it to exploit the technological lead it has acquired'.

Compatible technology is seen as one of the two necessary conditions for the development of interoperability. The other is a co-ordinated system of rules governing the rights and responsibilities of the various parties involved, notably card issuers and cardholders. At the same time, the Commission stresses the need to take care that the initiatives it wants to encourage do not have any anti-competitive aspects which might infringe the competition rules of the Treaty of Rome.

There has recently been a shift in emphasis of the Commission's strategy, which is examined later under the heading 'New Directions?'. However, the Commission's initiatives since 1987 on standardisation and – especially – on relations between card issuers and cardholders have already had considerable significance for consumers.

Standardisation

In June 1987, nearly six months after publication of the 'Ace' strategy document mentioned above, the Commission asked the European Committee for Standardisation (CEN) to undertake a co-ordinated programme of work which would lead to the drafting of a set of European standards for payment cards. A first workshop was held by

CEN in Brussels in April 1988, at which an 'Ad Hoc Group' was formed and asked to produce a report for discussion by a second workshop to be held the following year.

This second workshop was held in Brussels in May 1989. The report of the Ad Hoc Group concludes that there were no immediate and obvious gaps in the programme of standardisation being undertaken by the International Standards Organisation (ISO), so that European standardisation could in effect be accomplished by adopting ISO standards. However, it puts forward the controversial view that, while standards might deal with security *mechanisms* in payment systems, the issue of *levels* of security is not a matter for technical standardisation:

> 'The functions of CEN are limited to technical issues. Commercial issues are exclusively the concern of commercial organisations ... Security itself is fundamentally a commercial issue ... the selection of a level of security within particular applications must directly stem from the need to provide a competitive service, and thus be left to the workings of the market.' (CEN 1989)

The report of the Ad Hoc Group goes on to say that the responsibilities and rights of the financial institutions and retailers in relation to security are a matter for contractual arrangements between them, while consumers' interests are protected by the two Commission Recommendations of 1987 and 1988. The implication of this view is that consumers would have no guaranteed minimum level of security in electronic payment systems throughout the EC.

At the second CEN workshop in 1989, this majority view was strongly supported by representatives of the banking industry, but was criticised by representatives of other interests, including retailers, equipment suppliers and telecommunications bodies. Consumer representatives were especially critical of the view that payment cards standards should not cover levels of security. They argued that consumer confidence is an essential ingredient of the development of payment systems. Confidence needs to be based on a minimum level of security, so that consumers can be assured that transactions are free from fraud and error. They also pointed out that security is a major part of the Commission's telecommunications standardisation programme being implemented by the European Telecommunications Standards Institute (ETSI). The goal of interoperability would be much more difficult to achieve unless there was common agreement on the minimum level of security that electronic payments systems had to meet (Allix 1989: Mitchell 1989b).

The workshop did not draw up a detailed standardisation work programme, but proposed to CEN that it should focus on standardisation of smart cards, which include a number of other application fields as well as payments. This work is going ahead at the time of writing.

The situation remains unsatisfactory from the consumer viewpoint, as the CEN adoption of ISO standards for magnetic stripe cards fails to tackle the security issue. It is common knowledge that there are very variable levels of security in different electronic payment systems. The Ad Hoc Group's approach of levels of security being negotiated between the various parties involved is irrelevant so far as consumers are concerned – it is quite impracticable for consumers to negotiate levels of security with card issuers. The Commission must also be disappointed at this turn of events, as it had taken it for granted that European standardisation would include the need for effectively secure systems. The prospect of European payment systems which are physically and electronically compatible but geared to totally different security requirements must be seen as a setback to the achievement of interoperability.

The difficulty stems from the dominant role that representatives of the banks play in drawing up standards for payment systems. For example, the membership of the relevant ISO committees (nominated by national standards organisations) is drawn virtually entirely from the banking industry, and the CEN Ad Hoc Group had an overwhelming majority of banking and other financial institution members. Consumers are faced with the familiar situation of trying to make their views known in a forum dominated by the industry concerned – the one consolation in this instance being that retailers, equipment suppliers and telecommunications administrations find themselves in a similar 'minority' position.

What is the minimum level of security that consumers require from an electronic payments system? The following would seem to be the minimum requirements:

- There should be a positive identification of the cardholding consumer as the authorised user at the ATM or transaction terminal;
- The consumer's PIN or other unique identifier should be completely confidential to the cardholding consumer and the card issuing bank or other financial institution. Within the latter, electronic or other access to the PIN should be on a need-to-know

basis, so that the smallest possible number of people within the bank know the consumer's PIN. It should not be possible for other people or institutions (for example, the retailer where the transaction terminal is located) to obtain access to the PIN by electronic or other means. Among other things, this means that other people should not be able to read the PIN as the consumer is keying it in to the ATM or terminal;

- There should be absolute integrity within electronic payment systems – that is, information displayed or actions taken should be precisely as entered by the consumer. There should be no corruption or modification of the consumer's instruction;

- Electronic payment systems should ensure that the consumer's personal financial data is confidential to the consumer and to the bank or other financial institution holding the consumer's account against which the transaction is being debited;

- An audit trail should be available for the consumer if a transaction is disputed, in accordance with a provision of the Commission's Second Recommendation (see below);

- There should be discrete information and action boundaries between functions on multi-function smart cards. These should take account of the possibility that some ways in which the card is used may not be associated with electronic payments, but with other unrelated aspects of the consumer's life – for example, personal health information.

Until and unless consumers are assured that these minimum card security requirements are guaranteed throughout EC payments system networks, there will continue to be widespread scepticism about the repeated statements by banks that their electronic payment systems are absolutely secure, and proof against all errors and fraud. This scepticism is reinforced by a recent account, published by newspapers in Scotland, of how 40 consumers with accounts at the Clydesdale Bank had lost nearly £50,000 from their accounts as the result of unauthorised ATM withdrawals, allegedly made by a member of the bank staff (*Glasgow Herald* and *Daily Herald* 1 February 1991).

As banks seem to be unwilling to commit themselves to any published minimum security standard on a voluntary basis, the Commission should ensure that the issue is high on its own agenda. While voluntary standardisation is the preferred way of achieving this objective, an imposed solution should be considered if voluntary standards do not include minimum security levels. Otherwise, it will be difficult for the Commission's goal of interoperability to be achieved and consumers will remain sceptical about the claim by banks that electronic payment systems are entirely free from errors and fraud.

The Commission's First Recommendation

The Commission's first initiative in trying to achieve a reasonably consistent set of relations between card issuers, retailers and cardholders throughout the EC was to issue at the end of 1987 a Recommendation embodying a code of conduct on electronic payments (European Commission 1987b). This focuses primarily on relations between card issuers and retailers, but also includes some provisions affecting consumers. As a Recommendation, the code of conduct has no legal force and does not bind member states. It covers electronic payment systems that are triggered by the consumer's card being put into a terminal, but not paper-based card payment systems or cheque guarantee cards. The use of cards to withdraw cash from ATMs seem to be excluded from the coverage of the code, but this is not completely clear from the wording.

The code of conduct reiterates the Commission' objective of interoperability, first set out in the 'Ace' paper, and its clauses cover contracts, equipment and fairness of access to electronic payment systems for retailers. In view of the subsequent controversy over minimum levels of security, mentioned above, it is interesting that the code of conduct deals with data protection and mentions security as one of two conditions (convenience is the other) which have to be met if new electronic payment systems are to be developed for the benefit of consumers.

So far as contracts between card issuers and consumers are concerned, the code states that:

- They shall be in writing and must be the result of a prior application;
- They shall be drawn up in the official language of the member state in which the contract is made;
- Charges must be worked out 'in a transparent manner' and should not restrict competition;
- All conditions shall be freely negotiable and clearly stipulated;
- It should be clear how the contract can be ended.

There is little in these stipulations likely to resolve the persisting difficulties there are with card contracts, though the provision about conditions being freely negotiable seems to be honoured more in the breach than the observance.

In relation to data protection and security, the code lays down that electronic transmission of payment information '... must not in any circumstances prejudice the protection of privacy', adding that 'It shall be strictly limited to that laid down for cheques and transfers'. This is an attempt to align the principles of privacy for electronic payment systems with those already in place for other methods of payment. The code also states that 'Any problems whatsoever that arise in connection with the protection of information or with security must be openly acknowledged and cleared up at whatever stage in the contract between the parties'. This has no operational meaning in the context of contracts between card issuers and cardholders – as has been pointed out above, each card issuer issues a standardised contract which is not negotiated and is not negotiable.

The code also stipulates that 'Electronic payments are irreversible. An order given by means of a payment card shall be irrevocable and shall not be countermanded'. This parallels a French statutory provision (Article 22 of the Law of 11 July 1985) that a payment made by card is irrevocable, in the same way that payment by cheque in France is irrevocable. It is a detailed issue which continues to be troublesome, as its implications are unclear. From the consumer viewpoint, if the consumer authorises an electronic payment by mistake, or for the wrong amount, there should not be any obstacle to putting the error right by subsequent instructions.

A number of the code's provisions deal with fair competition in very general and unexceptionable terms. However, there is not much that is of specific and obvious benefit to consumers in the code. Also, it is not clear how its provisions should be interpreted in relation to multi-function cards, when one card function (for example, paying for petrol by using the card in an EFTPOS terminal) is covered by the code, while another (for example, using the card as a bank guarantee when paying by cheque) is not. There are no arrangements for monitoring compliance with the code or ensuring that it is implemented in member countries. Whatever its merits, it cannot be treated seriously as an instrument for dealing with the consumer protection aspects of payment cards.

The Commission's Second Recommendation

A year after its first initiative, the Commission launched a second Recommendation which focuses more closely on the relations between card issuers and cardholders (European Commission 1988b). The fact that the Commission's chosen instrument for action is a 'soft' Recommendation rather than a legally binding Directive is itself a matter of controversy. All the preparatory work was carried out with the intention that there would be a Directive adopted by the Council of Ministers, but at a late stage it was decided not to pursue this path.

The strong opposition of the three European Credit Sector Associations (ECSAs – European Banking Federation, Savings Bank Group of the EEC and Association of Co-operative Banks of the EC) to any Community legislation in this field may well have had a strong influence on the Commission's change of direction. In their comments on the draft Directive, they take issue with the need for a Directive:

> 'The first question ... is whether there is a need at all for legislation in the rapidly evolving area of payment systems ... the Federations believe that the laws of contract and of obligations already provide a suitable framework within the European legal jurisdictions for appropriate contractual arrangements to be entered into and adapted as systems evolve. Accordingly, the Federations do not believe that specific legislation is required in this area at the moment, and their comments on the draft text in no way imply backing for the concept of European legislation or guidelines in this field.' (ECSA 1988)

The switch from a Directive to a Recommendation has met with universal disapproval from the consumer side. At EC level, both the Commission's own Consumer Consultative Committee (CCC), the European Consumer Law Group and BEUC opposed the change. Their view has been widely shared by national consumer organisations, including Association des Consommateurs/Verbruikersunie (Belgium), Consumentenbond (Netherlands), Consumers in the European Community Group (UK) and National Consumer Council (UK).

The scope of this 1988 Recommendation is both wider and more specific than the 1987 Recommendation. It covers the use of cards to withdraw cash or make deposits in ATMs and to pay for goods and services in EFTPOS systems. It also includes electronic home banking and paper-based card payment systems but, as with the 1987 Recommendation, excludes the cheque guarantee function of plastic cards.

The main thrust of the Recommendation is to urge that within 12 months (that is, by 17 November 1989) card issuers and payments system providers should conduct their activities in accordance with a set of provisions set out in the Annex to the Recommendation. The most important of these are:

- Each card issuer shall draw up a full and fair written contract;
- The contract shall be written in plain language and in an easily readable form;
- The contract shall specify how charges are calculated;
- The contract shall specify whether debits and credits are instantaneous or, if not, the period of delay;
- The contract shall only be altered by agreement – however, the cardholder will be deemed to have accepted any changes that have been notified if she or he goes on using the card;
- The contract shall put the cardholder under an obligation to take all reasonable steps to keep the card and PIN safe and to notify the card issuer of the loss or theft of the card or PIN. Also, the cardholder should not note the PIN on the card or on anything which she or he usually keeps with the card;
- The contract shall put the cardholder under an obligation not to countermand an order which has been made by using the card;
- The contract shall state that if the cardholder complies with these requirements and doesn't otherwise act with extreme negligence or fraudulently, she or he shall not be financially liable after loss or theft is notified;
- The contract shall put the card issuer under an obligation not to disclose the PIN to anyone else;
- No payment card shall be issued unless the consumer asks for it and the contract operates from the time that the cardholder receives the card along with a copy of the contract;
- Cardholders shall keep records enabling operations to be traced and errors put right;
- In any dispute, the burden of proof shall be on the card issuer to show that the operation was carried out and recorded accurately and not affected by a breakdown or other deficiency;
- The cardholder shall be entitled to a transaction record;
- Each card issuer shall provide for a cardholder to notify loss or theft on a round-the-clock basis;
- Until loss or theft is notified, the cardholder's liability for use of the card is limited to 150 ECU 'for each event', but this liability

ceases after notification – unless the cardholder has acted with extreme negligence or fraudulently.

Some detailed aspects of these provisions are not completely clear, or provide the consumer with less than complete protection. For example, the obligation on the cardholding consumer not to countermand an order which has been given by using a card seems to leave open the possibility that the consumer would not be able to cancel a transaction where the wrong amount has been entered in. The shift in the burden of proof from the consumer to the card issuer does not go far enough – it is virtually impossible for a consumer to show that a disputed transaction was not authorised, so the card issuer should be under a clear obligation to prove that it was. Transaction records should be offered as a matter of course, not just when the consumer asks for them. In the limitation on liability of 150 ECU 'for each event', it is not clear whether the event refers to the loss or theft of a card or to each use of a lost or stolen card.

Despite these criticisms, there is no doubt that, taken together, the contents of this second Recommendation represent a significant advance on the existing protection available to consumers in member countries (other than Denmark, where the amended Danish Payment Cards Act applies).

What, then, has been done to follow up the Recommendation? One major step forward emphasised by Jean Allix is the focusing of responsibility clearly on the card issuer. He gives as an example the problems that might be faced by a French consumer using a payment card in an EFTPOS terminal in a Spanish retailer and noticing when the card account arrived that the amount charged for the transaction had an extra zero on the end. The transaction might involve as many as five different corporate bodies – the retailer, the retailer's bank, the telecom network operator, the international payment organisation (e.g. Visa, Eurocard) and the card issuer. The consumer would have no way of knowing where the error had occurred. The responsibility for detecting the mistake and making sure that it was put right should rest clearly with the card issuer, who has a contractual relationship with the consumer and has actually issued her or him with the piece of plastic (Allix 1990b).

The Banks' Code of Practice

In its Recommendation, the Commission warned that if, after 12 months, it found that implementation was unsatisfactory, it would 'take appropriate measures'. Shortly before the expiry of this period, on 24

October 1989, the three ECSA banking organisations submitted a proposed 'Code of Best Practice' to the Commission. This draft code was the subject of a number of meetings between the three ECSA banking organisations, the Commission and the CCC (Consumer Consultative Committee), in which the CCC was critical of the narrow scope of the draft code and of some of its detailed provisions.

An amended version of the draft code was submitted by the three ECSA banking organisations in January 1990. The CCC refused to endorse this amended version. It considered that the scope of the draft code was much more limited than the scope of the Commission Recommendation. For example, the draft code was confined to the use of payment cards in machines which read magnetic stripes – the consumer has no idea of whether any particular system or terminal used by a retailer comes within this definition or not, and so does not know whether or not the code applies. Another CCC criticism was that the draft code's failure to cover home banking or payment by telephone, when the card numbers are given over the telephone to the retailer but the card is not physically entered into a terminal. The CCC pointed out that the draft code applied only to banks and not to other types of card issuer, including retailers. A number of the draft code's detailed provisions were also criticised by the CCC as falling below the level of protection envisaged in the Commission's Recommendation (CCC 1990).

The three ECSA banking organisations made more amendments to the draft code and submitted a further revised version to the Commission in March 1990. The Commission's response stressed that if the 'soft' Recommendation approach that it had taken was to stand up as a credible alternative to a Directive, the code needed to reflect the provisions of the Recommendation more closely. In particular, the Commission focused on the following issues:

- The code should cover all payment card transactions, including paper-based ones, and should not be limited to the use of payment cards in ATM and EFTPOS systems;
- The draft code imposed unreasonably onerous duties on the cardholder if the card was lost or stolen;
- The code should make it clear that all new terminal equipment installed should offer the cardholder the option of a printed receipt/transaction record and that such a record should normally be given immediately and in any event within a reasonable time in a bank statement;

- The code should make it clear that the card issuer was responsible for any direct loss suffered by the cardholder as a result of a defect in a system or terminal.

The final version of the code drawn up by the three ECSA banking organisations, while unpublished at the time of writing, appears to have taken the substance of these points on board. It still does not cover home banking but does include the use of payment cards in paper-based as well as electronic systems. The use of payment cards to order and pay for goods and services over the telephone, for example when booking a hotel room or theatre tickets, is not referred to specifically in the text, and may still be a gap in terms of consumer protection (Allix 1990a). A number of other detailed issues seem to have been resolved – for example, the consumer's liability for any use of the card between the time when it is lost or stolen and notification of this to the card issuer is normally limited to a total of 150 ECU, rather than 150 ECU on each occasion when it is fraudulently used. Retail organisations are understood to be drawing up a comparable code.

After lengthy negotiations and pressure from consumer organisations, well outside the original timetable of the Commission Recommendation, it appears that the three ECSA banking organisations have now arrived at a code which conforms reasonably well with the spirit of the Recommendation. The outstanding question is whether the code will be effectively implemented.

The Prospects for Implementation

In November 1989, the time originally set by the Commission for implementation of its second Recommendation, the Netherlands consumer organisation, Consumentenbond, in conjunction with other member consumer organisations of BEUC, commissioned an appraisal of 190 sets of terms and conditions for payment cards issued by banks, other financial institutions and retailers throughout the EC. The study was carried out by the Molengraaff Institute for Private Law at the University of Utrecht (Knobbout-Bethlem 1990).

The aim of the study was to find out the extent of compliance with the Commission's Recommendation. The results show widespread disregard for key provisions in the Recommendation. For example:

- In the majority of instances, the cardholder's liability for the use of a lost or stolen card before notification to the card issuer of loss or theft is not limited to 150 ECU. Out of 122 bank cards examined, only 41 set the cardholder's liability at or below this level. Compliance ranges from being universal among banks in Germany and the Netherlands to complete non-compliance in Greece, Italy and Portugal. Out of 51 payment cards only eight respect the limit – all eight being issued in Germany and the UK. By contrast, charge cards generally comply;

- In a number of instances – 27 bank cards and 14 retailer cards – the cardholder's liability for use of a lost or stolen card does not cease when the card issuer is notified. The cardholder continues to be held liable. There are considerable differences from country to country. In France, Germany, the UK and the Netherlands, almost all cards comply with the provision of the Recommendation that the cardholder should not be liable after notification. The situation is variable in Spain, Ireland, Belgium and Luxembourg, while this aspect of the Recommendation is rarely complied with in Italy and Portugal. Again, charge cards generally comply;

- In relation to the burden of proof when a transaction is disputed, none of the card terms and conditions examined seems to be in line with the spirit of the Recommendation.

This unsatisfactory situation is reinforced by the apparent lack of any coherent attempt to follow up the Recommendation within the majority of member countries. The Netherlands is an exception, with negotiations taking place between Consumentenbond and the banks, while in France the Comité Consultatif is studying implementation. In the UK, the banks are engaged in producing a more general code of practice following the report of the Review Committee on Banking Services Law and Practice (1989).

The Commission insists that it is important for the three ECSA banking organisations to be able to show that banks are actually implementing the principles of the Recommendation. It has asked them to submit a full report on implementation 12 months after the final version of the code is ready. The banking organisations have responded that implementation is the responsibility of individual card-issuing banks and that, while they will try to provide the Commission with information from their members about implementation, they are not geared to carry out more detailed and regular monitoring.

At the time of writing, the prospects for effective implementation and monitoring of the code remain uncertain. As the Consumentenbond

/BEUC study shows, there is at present a wide gap between the principles of the Recommendation and the terms and conditions used by many card issuers. Given the whole history of this issue, and the repeated failure of the banks to take action without strong external pressure either from consumer bodies or from the Commission itself, it would not be safe to assume that implementation can be left to the banks themselves. Given the complexity and diversity of the retail trade, the implementation of any future code applying to retail card issuers is likely to be even more problematic. The Commission will need to ensure that there is an effective monitoring system, that sanctions are available to be used against institutions that fail to comply, and that if there continues to be widespread non-compliance the Recommendation will be replaced by a legally binding Directive.

Retail Codes

An advisory body of the Commission, the Committee on Commerce and Distribution, has set itself the task of drawing up a code of practice on the relations between card issuers and retailers, which is designed to implement the Commission's first Recommendation (Committee on Commerce and Distribution 1991b). Simultaneously, the same Committee is drafting a code of practice on the relations between retailers – as card issuers – and consumers, which is rooted in the Commission's second Recommendation. The problems of monitoring and enforcing adherence by retailers to a code of this kind would seem to be even greater than with the banks (Committee on Commerce and Distribution 1991c).

Competition Rules

When the consumer uses a plastic card to withdraw cash from an ATM, it is a relatively straightforward banking transaction. However, the development of electronic payment systems which make it possible for consumers to pay for goods and services by putting a credit or debit card in a terminal is a much more complicated business, which may involve a number of financial and other institutions. The banks' perception is that the new payment and money transmission systems are an old function in a new guise, and should remain under their control. Retailers, non-bank card issuers and others do not share this perception. They are anxious that agreements among banks will exclude them from participating fully in the development of new payment systems and are sensitive to any moves by the banks to keep them out. There is therefore a continuing struggle for power in which, at European level, the Commission plays a crucial role.

What is the consumer interest in an extremely complex and rapidly changing situation? The consumer advantage seems to lie clearly in ensuring that electronic payment systems are as open as possible, with access for banks and other institutions to compete in providing cards and services to individual consumers. While recognising that some degree of co-operation among institutions may be necessary, any agreement which limits competition (for example, by price discrimination or by excluding certain types of institution) without providing consumers with compensatory benefits should be forbidden.

What is the European Commission's role? There are two Articles of the Treaty of Rome which deal with competition. Article 85 forbids any collusion designed to prevent, restrict or distort competition, while Article 86 prohibits abuse of a dominant position. Not all collusive agreements are automatically prohibited. There are powers for the Commission to grant an exemption under Article 85(3) for an agreement:

> '... which contributes to improving the production of goods or to promoting technical or economic progress, while allowing consumers a fair share of the resulting benefit, and which does not:
> (a) impose on the undertakings concerned restrictions which are not indispensable to the attainment of these objectives;
> (b) afford such undertakings the possibility of eliminating competition in respect of a substantial part of the products in question.'

The consumer interest is therefore recognised, though there is nothing specific about how to measure whether or not consumers get a fair share of the resulting benefit from an anti-competitive agreement. It is not something which the Commission has tackled in a very methodical way in its various decisions under Article 85(3) – there is invariably a dearth of quantitative information.

The 'Accord'

In 1987, the European Council for Payment Systems (a group of 40 banking organisations from EC countries, Austria, Finland, Norway, Sweden and Switzerland) responded to the Commission's 'Ace' strategy by launching an *Accord for Bank Card Usage* (ECPS 1987). The object of the Accord is to achieve 'reciprocity' of payment cards throughout Europe. Though at first sight very similar, the ECPS concept of reciprocity in fact differs significantly from the Commission's concept of interoperability. The Commission's aim is to achieve interoperability for all payment cards – or, at least, the vast bulk of them. The ECPS arrangement is limited to cards which the ECPS member banks in each country designate for use in other European countries. It covers paper-based as well as electronic payment systems and would involve a common recognition symbol on designated cards, ATMs and bank branches, as well as participating retailers. It was intended that a common charging structure would be developed.

While implementation of the Accord might have speeded up the mutual recognition and acceptance of different payment cards throughout the EC and neighbouring participating countries, it would have had a number of consumer disadvantages, including the following:

• Direct participation in the Accord would be limited to banks. There is no provision for building societies or other financial institutions such as Diners Club and American Express to take part. It would therefore be an exclusive network limiting consumer choice;

• The Accord would be limited to European banks, excluding banks based elsewhere which are authorised to offer banking services in European countries. This not only conflicts with the Second Banking Co-ordination Directive but would create a protectionist barrier in world trade in financial services;

• The Accord would be based on each national group of banks within the ECPS taking collective decisions about, for example, the number of designated ATMs in its country, the number of contracted retailers, and similar matters. This would have implications for national competition and anti-trust policies within each country;

• While each participating bank would be free to decide its own charges to cardholding consumers, there would be a harmonised structure of inter-bank charges. This would have implications for competition and anti-trust policies at EC and national levels.

The original Accord was an expression of intent to reach an agreement, rather than a formal agreement. Nevertheless, it has come under the scrutiny of the Commission's Directorate-General for Competition (DG IV). It seems unlikely that it will survive in anything like its original form, despite statements by ECPS that it is not dead. If an obituary notice is needed, in the spirit of not speaking ill of the dead it can be said that the Accord has played a valuable – though unintended – role in highlighting the scope for anti-competitive agreements in developing payment systems and in alerting the Commission to the need to integrate its competition role with its payment systems strategy. For example, what is fair and what is unfair in the rules governing admission to payment system networks? Should discrimination on grounds of the type or size of institution – or its 'nationality' – be allowed? Is it anti-competitive for the rules of any one payment system organisation to forbid participating member institutions from joining other systems? What kind of agreements on common tariffs are admissible?

New Directions?

The Commission's original 'Ace' document was published in 1987. There have been many changes since then – four years is a long time in current perspectives of payment systems. The commercial and technical constraints to the achievement of interoperability are clearer now than they were then. In commercial terms, most card issuers fly either the Visa or the Mastercard flag (some fly both, in the sense that they offer consumers a choice of a Visa card or a Mastercard), although American Express and Diners Club make tactical agreements with different financial institutions. Unless there is a major change, EC-wide interoperability looks as if it will work out as two or more separate systems. In technical terms, as has been explained above, standardisation of magnetic stripe cards is limited to physical compatibility, leaving security levels to be privately negotiated between participants – other than consumers, of course, who have no choice but to accept the unknown levels of security chosen by their card issuers.

Meanwhile, in the field of telecommunications, the Commission's emphasis on Open Network Provision (ONP) has opened up new possibilities. The dual aim of ONP is to stimulate the development of new telecommunications services and to promote fair competition (European Commission 1987c and 1988c). This involves open access to the public telecommunications network and means that in time all elements in payment systems will be mutually compatible – for example, a retailer could choose any make of terminal in the knowledge that it would fit against the network. This adds a new dimension to the Commission's goal of card interoperability and reinforces the Commission's original view of electronic EC payment systems as a series of interconnected networks – the equivalent for electronic payments of a Community-wide complex of interconnected motorway networks for road transport. The policy issue that the Commission must face is whether this will come about through market forces or whether it will need a more structured framework imposed or stimulated by the Commission itself.

Prepaid Payment Cards

Another new development which has begun to attract the attention of the Commission is that of prepaid payment cards. These have been introduced by a number of telephone administrations throughout the world in conjunction with public callboxes which accept such cards rather than cash. British Telecom (BT) and Mercury in the UK, RTT in Belgium and New Zealand Telecom are examples of telephone administrations which use magnetic stripe cards which are sold in advance to consumers. For example, in the UK the consumer can buy for £5 a card which can be used to pay for 50 timed telephone call 'units'. The number of unused units on the card is displayed visually on the public callbox telephone at the time a call is being made.

In Japan, where cash is still the predominant method of payment and credit cards are not widely used, prepaid cards are becoming big business. The first one was introduced by Nippon Telegraph and Telephone (NTT) in 1982 and by March 1988 over 440 million telephone cards had been sold, worth the equivalent of 1.5 billion ECU. They are now issued by other suppliers of goods and services, including petrol stations, supermarkets and cinemas (*Electronic Payments International* April 1989).

France Télécom and Deutsche Bundespost have introduced prepaid card systems based on smart card technology and this may be the way that future developments lie. Smart cards may have more than one application built into the card – for example, the same card might be used for making telephone calls, paying for bus or train journeys and paying motorway or bridge tolls.

Banks are also becoming interested in the possibilities of offering prepaid cards to their customers. Cash is still far and away the most widely used form of payment. In the UK and France, cards and cheques still only account for some 15 per cent of all retail transactions and in other EC countries the proportion is less than this. Banks see the possibility of replacing cash transactions by prepaid card transactions, which would reduce the considerable costs involved in handling and processing large quantities of cash through the banking and retailing systems (INTAMIC 1990).

The European Commission has not so far issued any public policy proposals on the policy implications of the use of prepaid payment cards in the single market. As prepaid cards are anonymous and not personalised, they avoid some of the difficulties attached to the use of other forms of payment card, which have been dealt with above. They do not appear to be covered by the Commission's first or second Recommendations or by the code of practice being drawn up by the three ECSA banking organisations. There are, however, two consumer issues. First, when they buy prepaid cards, consumers are in effect making an interest-free deposit with the card issuer. This may not amount to much on any individual card, but large numbers of cards would make a dramatic improvement to the cash flow of the card issuer. Also, card issuers make surplus profits from prepaid cards that are lost or not fully used – the cards are not refundable. If the consumer has a prepaid card stolen, then she or he bears the loss, not the card issuer (Mitchell 1989a).

Second, prepaid card issuers are in effect acting as deposit-taking institutions, but are not subject to prudential regulation unless they are banks. There are no safeguards against them going out of business and no redress for consumers who have bought prepaid cards if they do. The prospect in Japan of different kinds of businesses coming together to issue multi-purpose prepaid cards which could be used for a variety of different payment applications has prompted the Japanese Ministry of Finance to consider whether or not they should be subject to regulation. The outcome is that legislation has been introduced with effect from 1 October 1990 which includes the following provisions:

- Issuers of prepaid cards must register with the Ministry of Finance when the unused prepaid amount exceeds the equivalent of c.50,000 ECU. At the end of every March and September they are required to deposit or lodge a guarantee with the Ministry for at least 50 per cent of the unused amount. The effect of this is to transfer some of the benefits of the improved cash flow from the card issuers to the government;
- Organisations issuing prepaid cards to their employees are required to report details to the Ministry of Finance every March and September when the unused prepaid amount reaches the equivalent of 35,000 ECU;

- A declaration of the above intent must be shown on the prepaid card;
- Prepaid card issuers must observe various regulations on the records and documents that should be kept;
- A prepaid card issuers' association shall be set up for the protection of consumers and to maintain the integrity of the cards that are issued, to operate under regulations laid down by the government (INTAMIC 1990).

If the use of multi-application prepaid cards spreads within the EC, then the Commission will need to pay attention to the regulatory and consumer protection issues which have been dealt with in this Japanese legislation.

The Consumer Agenda
From the consumer viewpoint, there are three outstanding issues:

- Consumers need to have confidence that electronic payment systems are free from fraud and error and that their money is not at risk. The failure to date of the voluntary standardisation programme to ensure that there is a minimum level of security for magnetic stripe payment cards and their associated systems is unacceptable. The Commission needs to address this problem as a matter of urgency, not least to ensure that one of the necessary conditions for the achievement of interoperability is met;
- While it seems that the code of practice prepared by the three ECSA banking organisations is now reasonably consistent with the letter and spirit of the Commission's second Recommendation, attention should now be paid to making sure that it is properly implemented and monitored. The same applies to other kinds of financial institution and to retailers. If these and comparable provisions are not put into effect fully and rapidly by the whole spectrum of card issuers, the Commission should issue a legally binding Directive to make sure that consumers are properly protected;
- The growing use of prepaid payment cards, and their likely spread from telephone administrations to other kinds of issuing organisation, poses a potential problem. A wide variety of organisations might in effect become involved in accepting deposits from consumers, without consumers having any assurance that their deposits (that is, the outstanding value stored

in the cards for which they have paid in advance) will be redeemable. A legal solution to this has been found in Japan and the Commission should consider what needs to be done in the EC.

Cross-border Payments

Consumers travelling in other EC countries need to be able to make on-the-spot payments for the goods and services they buy. Without travelling abroad, consumers may want to make regular or one-off payments to consumers living in other countries, or to buy goods and services from abroad. Consumers may receive regular or one-off payments from other countries, ranging from a monthly pension to a birthday present. The goal of achieving a single market for financial services means that it should be just as easy for a consumer to make payments in or to another EC country as it is within her or his own country. The main relevant payment methods are cash, payment cards, cheques (including travellers' cheques and Eurocheques) and bank transfers. The implications of the single market for consumers' use of each of these payment methods are examined below.

Cash

There is a cost to using cash for cross-border payments. The consumer buying a foreign currency has in effect to pay for the margin between the buying and selling rate for the currency, and sometimes a commission fee as well. One study showed that a consumer travelling round all EC member countries lost almost half her or his initial cash through exchange rate margins and commissions (BEUC 1988c). The consumer may also suffer a loss if the exchange rate moves adversely while holding cash in a foreign currency – though there is the corresponding possibility of a gain if the exchange rate moves favourably.

What impact will the single market for financial services have on these costs? The short-term answer must be none. However, the limits to exchange rate fluctuations of currencies within the Exchange Rate Mechanism (ERM) of the European Monetary System (EMS) limit the potential loss or gain from exchange rate movements. This element would be eliminated completely by the irrevocable fixing of EC exchange rates in the final stage of Economic and Monetary Union (EMU). If and when there is ever a single European currency, the costs involved in buying and selling foreign currencies would also disappear, as the single currency would be valid tender throughout the EC. The European Commission estimates that the total savings from all sources to consumers stemming from the introduction of a single European currency would amount to 15 billion ECU p.a. (European Commission 1990e).

Payment Cards

The consumer advantages and problems associated with the use of payment cards, as well as the initiatives taken by the Commission, have been dealt with in the chapter on Payment Cards. So far as cross-border use and payments are concerned, the Commission's policy has been to achieve the interoperability of cards, so that a card issued in any one EC country may be used in ATMs and payment terminals in other member countries. It has stimulated standardisation work within the European standardisation body CEN, as technical compatibility of cards and card terminals is a necessary though not a sufficient condition for interoperability. Standards for magnetic stripe cards developed by ISO have been adopted as European standards, while CEN is currently considering standards for smart cards, which may be used for other purposes (for example, recording an individual's personal health data) as well as for payments.

The commercial aspects of interoperability have seen a growing interconnection of ATM networks, though the situation is still patchy, as the table overleaf shows

The table demonstrates that the Commission's goal of interoperability is still a long way from being achieved so far as cash withdrawals are concerned. Consumers are not yet in a position where they can depend on being able to use their ATM cards to obtain cash when travelling in other EC countries, though the situation is improving year by year. For example, the total of ATMs that will accept Eurocheque cards is forecast at 33,153 by summer 1991. Also, savings banks in 11 EC countries now have interoperable ATMs and by end-1990 American Express cards could be used to withdraw cash from any of 11,500 ATMs throughout the EC.

Interconnection of ATM Networks (Spring 1990)

	No. of ATMs	Eurocard	open to Eurocheque	Visa
Belgium	850	500	640	500
Denmark	176	–	176	176
Germany	7,400	–	900	–
Greece	130	–	–	72
France	12,367	1,124	1,000	4,941
Ireland	346	–	–	180
Italy	5,200	397	1,450	796
Luxembourg	73	–	53	20
Netherlands	1,800	–	1,800	–
Portugal	550	550	550	550
Spain	12,500	4,300	4,400	7,000
UK	15,982	–	1,868	7,940
Total EC	57,374	6,871	12,837	22,175

(*Source:* Card Organisations. Figures exclude bilateral interconnection agreements between individual financial institutions)

Credit and charge cards are increasingly used as a convenient way of buying goods and services in other EC countries, as well as a way of getting cash. There is considerable variation between countries in the number and type of outlet at which different credit and charge cards are accepted in payment for goods and services. One consumer issue which has recently come to light is that many credit cards in effect charge the consumer a concealed fee by giving a worse exchange rate than they themselves receive. In a study carried out by the UK Consumers' Association, six Visa card issuing UK banks (Yorkshire, Midland, Bank of Scotland, Co-operative, TSB and Barclaycard) included in the exchange rate applied to credit card transactions 'fees', ranging from 0.5 per cent to 2.75 per cent of the value of the transaction. Diners Club applied a 'conversion fee' of 1 per cent. The existence of these 'fees' was not disclosed either generally in the terms and conditions of credit card use or specifically in relation to individual transactions. American Express applied a fee of 1 per cent on top of the tourist exchange rate (as distinct from the more favourable bulk or wholesale exchange rate), but states this in its terms and conditions (*Which?* April 1990). The failure to reveal to the consumer the existence of fees of this kind in relation to cross-border payments surely breaches the Commission Recommendation on transparency, dealt with in more detail later (European Commission 1990c).

The cross-border use of debit cards is as yet undeveloped. However, it is reported that one of the two leading UK debit cards, Switch, may constitute a major part of the plans being developed by Eurocard /MasterCard and Eurocheque for an international framework within which debit cards could be used at EFTPOS terminals throughout the EC (*Retail Banker International* 17 December 1990).

Cheques

Using an ordinary cheque drawn in the payer's local currency to make a cross-border payment may well involve the payee in delay while the cheque is cleared and in charges for the cost of clearing and currency conversion. These charges are impossible to forecast, so the payer does not know in advance how much money the payee will be left with after they have been deducted. This uncertainty, and the proportionally high cost of charges for low value payments, severely limits the usefulness of ordinary cheques as a way of making cross-border payments. Doubt has been expressed as to whether ordinary cheques will remain relevant for cross-border payments – if they do, then the problems to be tackled in improving their efficiency as an instrument for cross-border payment are very similar to those encountered with bank transfers, dealt with below.

Travellers' Cheques

Travellers' cheques have long been established as a convenient method for making on-the-spot payments when travelling abroad and for obtaining cash in local currency. Their advantage over cash is that, if lost or stolen, they may be replaced – and there is no loss to the consumer. They are issued by banks and by other institutions concerned with travel and payments, such as American Express and Thomas Cook.

In the UK, a minority of issuers do not charge commission, though the going rate is 1 per cent of the value of the cheques. A charge may be made when cashing a travellers' cheque abroad if the cheque is not in the local currency – for example, cashing a sterling travellers' cheque in France. The consumer may be faced with a loss on returning home when converting back unused foreign currency travellers' cheques.

The single European market seems unlikely to have a major short-term impact on travellers' cheques, which have not yet been a focus for the Commission's attention. This may change at some time in the future. Reflecting on the fact that the Commission's discussion paper on cross-border payments does not deal with travellers' cheques, a senior official notes that:

> 'We had thought that these were instruments of such longstanding international tradition, that measures promoting the integration of the EC internal payments market could not add much to their efficiency; nevertheless, they should not be overlooked in the forthcoming discussion, as they are one facet of a market in which overall competition, also between various kinds of payment instruments, is very fierce indeed.' (Troberg 1990)

Eurocheques

The search for a more efficient medium of payment led a number of financial institutions to set up the Eurocheque organisation, which provides a system for cross-border cheque clearing and settlement. Member banks issue uniform Eurocheques and Eurocheque guarantee cards, which may also be used to withdraw cash from ATMs. In 1989, more than 42 million Eurocheques were issued, worth 5.6 billion ECU. Eurocheques are available in most EC countries but seem to be most popular with German, Dutch and Belgian consumers – especially when they are on holiday in the mediterranean countries. Use of Eurocheque guarantee cards for obtaining cash is increasing: by Spring 1990 there were 12,837 ATMs throughout the EC at which Eurocheque cards could be used to withdraw cash.

When used in conjunction with a guarantee card, a Eurocheque is guaranteed by the issuing bank up to a ceiling in local currency roughly equivalent to 170 ECU (300 Swiss francs). The system for clearing Eurocheques of less than 340 ECU (600 Swiss francs) involves a commission being charged by the accepting bank to the issuing bank of a maximum of 1.6 per cent of the value of the cheque (subject to a minimum equivalent to 2 Swiss francs). A variable clearing centre charge may also be levied. If the Eurocheque is for more than the equivalent of 340 ECU, it is settled bilaterally between the accepting bank and the issuing bank, and may be subject to appreciably higher charges which are not known in advance.

In most countries, any charges in connection with the use of Eurocheques are paid by the payer. There is no charge to the payee. However, in France accepting banks charge the payee an extra fee. In anticipation of this, many French retailers levy a charge on the consumer who pays by Eurocheque.

The current Eurocheque arrangements came into force on 1 May 1981 and were subjected to scrutiny by the European Commission to see whether or not they were anti-competitive. The Commission ruled that the Eurocheque system involved restrictive practices which were explicitly caught by Article 85(1) of the Treaty of Rome, in that it inhibited competition between member banks in the encashment of Eurocheques, because of the standardisation of inter-bank commission payments. The standardisation of cheque guarantee levels was also ruled to be a restriction on competition.

However the Eurocheque arrangements were granted an exemption under Article 85(3), in that they contributed to the improvement of payment facilities within the EC, that a fair share of the resulting benefits went to Eurocheque users, that the restrictions were indispensable to the proper functioning of the Eurocheque system, and that they did not eliminate competition in respect of a substantial part of international means of payment – consumers still had available the alternative payment methods of cash, travellers' cheques and credit cards. In the Regulation implementing its decision, the Commission stipulated that issuing banks should tell consumers in detail about the costs of using Eurocheques abroad. Also, accepting banks should tell consumers about the cost of cashing Eurocheques (European Commission 1984).

The Eurocheque arrangements were due to run for an initial period of five years, that is until 30 April 1986. The Eurocheque organisation has asked for a renewal of the exemption and there have been protracted discussions about new arrangements and their relationship with the European Commission's competition policy. In September 1990, the Commission sent a statement of objections, which included the following points:

- In practice, the permitted 'maximum' inter-bank commission rate of 1.6 per cent of the value is virtually always the rate that is charged to the consumer paying by Eurocheque. Also, if a Eurocheque guarantee card is used to withdraw cash at an ATM in another country, there is a standard inter-bank commission of 0.25 per cent of the value of the withdrawal charged, with a minimum of the equivalent of 2.75 Swiss francs;
- Consumers are not given enough information about the charges they will incur when using Eurocheques abroad;
- The low maximum value (i.e. the equivalent of roughly 340 ECU) for Eurocheques cleared through the normal Eurocheque clearing system is a disadvantage to many consumers who need to pay larger amounts for relatively straightforward transactions.

These issues are all of direct concern to individual consumers, as is the 'double charging' – of the payee as well as the payer – on Eurocheques which are cashed or deposited in France. The Eurocheque organisation's response to the Commission's criticisms is under consideration at the time of writing.

Bank Transfers

Many consumers have had personal experience of the delay and expense which can be involved in making or receiving a cross-border bank transfer within the EC, or being told that it is not worth making such a transfer because the costs involved would cancel out the value to be transferred. The time taken and the costs involved give every appearance of being random and outside the consumer's control. Only too often, it is not possible for the consumer to obtain clear information about the quickest and cheapest way of making cross-border transfers. One UK consumer cites as an example trying to pay in Belgian francs a bill from a Brussels-based organisation and being sent by her bank a form with an explanation that paying this way was very expensive: there was, however, no explanation either of the precise cost or what alternative cheaper payment methods were available (personal letter to author).

Consumer Problems

Systematic evidence is provided in a study carried out by Bureau Européen des Unions de Consommateurs (BEUC 1988b), which included a test survey of 144 cross-border bank transfers within the EC, in which a consumer instructed her or his bank to transfer the equivalent of 100 ECU to a designated bank account in another EC member country. While many transfers were effected quickly and without difficulty, three took as long as two and a half, three and five months respectively. Two transfers did not reach their destination, despite being debited against the payer's account. The survey revealed a level of quality control in the provision of this service which is not acceptable and confirmed to many consumers that their own unfortunate experiences were by no means atypical.

Charges on payments of 100 ECU averaged 9 per cent to the payer, but these were sometimes supplemented by charges levied on the payee, despite the payer having instructed her or his bank to ensure that this did not happen. In the words of the report, '... the payee's bank almost *automatically* makes charges on incoming payments, without checking whether the charges have already been paid abroad by the payer'. Consumers are therefore often subject to triple jeopardy – the payer pays her or his own charges, plus the payee's charges – which are then levied a second time on the payee. Furthermore, the payee is not informed through the banking system that the payer has paid all charges and is faced with having to try to recover the money which has been deducted by the bank at the time value was credited. This situation is not only unacceptable to consumers – it verges on malpractice. Comparable double charging for goods and services outside the banking industry would almost certainly result in legal action against the supplier.

This situation contrasts markedly with arrangements for making transfer payments within any one country, which are frequently efficient. Intra-national transfer payments can be made quickly and cheaply in many EC member countries. Quite apart from the trouble and inconvenience which consumers often have to suffer in the present cross-border system, the high cost of relatively small cross-border transfers represents an obstacle to cross-border trade in goods and services and is a barrier to the development of the single market.

Improved Transparency
The European Commission's first attempt to deal with this unsatisfactory situation was to adopt on 14 February 1990 a *Recommendation on the Transparency of Banking Conditions Relating to Cross-border Financial Transactions* (European Commission 1990c). The Recommendation is described as a first step in a series of measures to improve the position of consumers who wish to transfer money across an internal EC border, including paying for goods or services in an EC country other than their own – it does not deal with cheques, payment cards or cash payments.

The background to the Recommendation makes it clear that the Commission's definition of 'transparency' is not limited to price information in the strict sense. It also includes information about the methods and timing of transfers, and procedures for dealing with complaints from consumers. The Recommendation calls on banks throughout the EC to respect six principles, which cover the following ground:

• Easily understandable and readily available information for consumers explaining the cost, timing and procedures used for cross-border transfers;

- In any specific transfer, both the payer and payee should get a detailed statement setting out the exchange rate used and any charges and fees;
- Information to the payer about the allocation of charges and fees between payer and payee;
- Each bank or other financial institution involved in a transfer should deal with it within two working days of receiving the funds to be transferred, unless it notifies its refusal to execute the transfer – any delay would entitle the payer to obtain a refund of part of the transfer costs;
- The payee's bank should credit the money to her or his account not later than the working day after it receives the funds;
- Each bank involved in a cross-border transaction should be capable of dealing rapidly with any complaint by the payer or payee – with provision for an independent national complaints body to deal with the complaint if no action has been taken on a complaint within three months.

An extensive critique of the scope and contents of the Recommendation was made at the draft stage by the Consumer Consultative Committee (CCC), an advisory body to the European Commission. In addition to detailed comments on the proposed text, the CCC notes that this is the first occasion on which the Commission has paid any attention to the transparency of banking conditions. It goes on to point out the paradox that in some EC countries implementation of the Recommendation would mean that consumers would be given information about the costs and timing of cross-border transfers while they would still not have comparable information about transfers within their own countries. The CCC urges the Commission not to confine its attention to cross-border transfers, but to look more broadly both at the transparency of banking charges and conditions and at the free circulation of all forms of payment methods, including cheques, payment cards and cash, within the single market (Consumer Consultative Committee 1989).

As with the Commission's work on payment cards, mentioned above, an initiative conceived as a draft of a legally binding Directive has eventually seen the light of day as a non-binding Recommendation made under Article 155 of the Treaty of Rome. The ostensive reason for this given by the Commission is that it does not appear 'expedient' to ask member states which already have relevant legislation to amend this to include new provisions relating solely to cross-border transfers. Also, some member states were said to want '... to retain proven co-operation procedures in order to improve relations between financial institutions and users' (European Commission 1990c).

The disadvantage of this approach so far as consumers are concerned is that little or no attention may be paid to a Commission Recommendation. Individual banks, banking organisations and member states themselves do not necessarily feel that they are under any obligation to comply with a non-binding Recommendation, reasoning that if the Commission was serious about an issue it would have followed the path of preparing a binding Directive for adoption by the Council of Ministers. A Recommendation may therefore give the impression that something has been done to tackle a problem when in fact the real situation remains unchanged.

Improved Cross-border Payment Systems

The softness of the Commission's approach on transparency of cross-frontier transfers may have lulled banks and other financial institutions into a false sense of complacency. On 26 September 1990, the Commission launched a discussion paper on *Making Payments in the Internal Market* (European Commission 1990e). This surveys the whole field of cross-border payments – cash, transfers, cheques and payment cards. It stresses that at Community level 'the benefits of the internal market will only be fully realised if systems for effecting cross-frontier payments operate as effectively as those at national level'. Unusually for a document coming from DG XV, it underlines the importance of having systems which meet the needs of individual consumers and small businesses, as well as large corporate institutions.

The Commission recognises that within each member country, there have been improvements in the range and efficiency of payment systems, largely as a result of initiatives by banks, and expresses the intention of ensuring that comparable systems are developed for cross-border payments. It sets out seven characteristics that efficient EC cross-border payment systems should have. They should:

- Speedily effect payments according to clear timetables which are respected in all but exceptional circumstances;
- Ensure that the (explicit and implicit) costs for those using them are reasonable, known in advance and subject to the maximum extent to competitive forces;

- Clearly delineate the rights, responsibilities and liabilities of all parties concerned;
- Meet high standards of security, robustness and integrity;
- Be subject to regular monitoring and the control of the risks associated with them;
- Not incorporate unnecessary restrictions e.g. on the amount that can be paid over;
- Be useable for cross-border payments, including those outside the Community.

These characteristics, so far as they go, are likely to get the support of consumers. However, the UK Consumers in the European Community Group (CECG) points to a number of gaps. A consumer faced with a dispute about a delayed transaction or about unreasonable charges may well have no avenue of redress other than the courts, often an impracticable way forward, especially when small amounts of money are involved. Also, CECG stresses the need not merely for a clear delineation of the rights, responsibilities and liabilities of those involved, but for fairness in the terms of contracts, which experience has shown cannot be taken for granted in the banking sector. CECG supports the reference to regular monitoring and asks the Commission to ensure that adequate resources are available for this, citing the lack of any Commission-funded monitoring of the Recommendation on payment cards as the reason for scepticism about any serious commitment to this activity (Consumers in the European Community Group 1990a).

The Commission's analysis of the deficiencies of the present situation focuses on the inadequacies, in this context, of the correspondent banking system, which means that a number of banks may be involved in what remains often a manual – and therefore expensive – transaction, in which neither costs nor timing are necessarily known in advance. The Commission points to the need to find some way to link national ACHs (Automated Clearing Houses), so that payments could be sent between member states more cheaply and more quickly than now, using less manual processing. Various options are set out in the discussion document and the Commission proposes a collaborative framework with central banks, banks and other interested parties to find the best way forward and to monitor progress, in the form of a Payment Systems Co-ordinating Group which would bring together '… central banks, banks and all other interested parties'. (In fact, in April 1991 the Commission set up two advisory bodies, a Payment Systems Technical Development Group, with its membership drawn from the banks, and a Payment Systems Users' Liaison Group, whose membership includes representatives of banks, small and medium sized enterprises, retailers and consumers).

The Commissioner responsible, Sir Leon Brittan, has underlined the strength of the Commission's determination to improve the present situation and has set the Commission's objectives in the context of monetary union as well as the single market for financial services. In a speech delivered to a Commission conference on 15 October 1990, he said:

> '... all too often making a cross-border transfer appears complicated, expensive and slow. Even if there is a better way to make a cross-border payment than the one which he has chosen, the customer cannot always readily obtain the necessary information to make an informed choice ... Greater transparency is the right starting point. But it seemed to us useful and necessary to go further than this and to bring the whole question of the organisation of payment systems into the foreground ... to achieve the great commercial benefits of a single currency in a single market we must unlock our payment systems from their current national structures and set them firmly in a European context.' (Brittan 1990b)

The Banks' Reaction

At this same conference, the banks expressed undisguised hostility to what they saw as the Commission's interference in matters which should be left to them to sort out. The President of the European Council for Payment Systems (ECPS), Gabriel Pallez, is reported as saying that current methods for making cross-border payments seemed to meet the needs of consumers and that it was not the Commission's function to impose new arrangements on the banks. A German banker warned that any initiative by the Commission should not be allowed to impinge on the autonomy of individual banks, both in respect of charges for cross-border payments and the functioning of the present correspondent banking system (*European Banker* 29 October 1990). There was strong resistance by some banking representatives to participation of consumer representatives in the conference and a public threat by one German banker that if consumer representatives were invited to future discussions, the banks would not take part (author's observation).

The formal response of the European Banking Federation (EBF) to the Commission's discussion paper is more measured in tone but gives little ground on the substance of the issues. It welcomes the Commission's initiative '... to prompt exchanges of views among specialists in this field' but emphasises that future developments in payment systems '... should not be allowed to impinge upon the autonomy of individual financial institutions with regard to their decisions'. The EBF says that, so far as individual consumers are concerned, on-the-spot payments are largely covered by existing payment methods of cash, travellers' cheques, payment cards and Eurocheques. It also claims that there are few difficulties with recurring payments, such as pensions, to consumers living abroad, and says that the big problem is with non-recurring, low-value transfers initiated by consumers. These are said to be cumbersome, involving a high work load which produces little revenue, and only constitute a minor part of the global market.

The EBF then goes on to refer to a study (unpublished) carried out by some ACHs in 1989 intended to devise a simple transfer system to serve this particular market, based on a linkage between ACHs. It says that no technically or economically viable solution was found with the result that the ACHs decided not to proceed with their planned link-up.

More broadly, the EBF raises a number of fundamental questions about the way forward:

- Should any solution be European or global?
- Should public or private sector solutions be preferred?
- Which comes first, monetary union or a uniform payment system?
- Fixed or market prices?
- Where do the interests of the banks lie?
- Should there be a single, pan-EC system, or a two-speed one which takes account of the varying sophistication of national payments systems?
- Should developments be imposed or left to the banks to work out co-operatively?

In expressing its willingness to study a proposal for the linkage of ACHs, the EBF points to the technical and economic problems to be overcome and reiterates that any new Europe-wide system for bulk payment transactions should be an alternative to and not a substitute for the correspondent banking system. It also raises doubts about the purpose, membership and constitution of the Payment Systems Co-ordinating Group proposed by the Commission and stresses that such a group should not be set up as a decision-making body (European Banking Federation 1990).

The Consumer Agenda

Where does the consumer interest lie in this unfinished and un-expectedly controversial saga? There is anecdotal and systematic evidence that one-off, low value cross-border bank transfers may be expensive and delayed, and that consumers are not given adequate information about the most efficient ways of making such transfers. The levels of service to be aimed at should be that cross-border transfers within the EC should not be more expensive or take any longer than transfers within anyone country. If alternative methods are available, consumers should be given enough information to enable them to take sensible decisions about which method to use.

The consumer perspective must therefore be that the Commission is fully justified in appraising present arrangements and satisfying itself that substantial improvements are put in hand. The argument put forward by some bank representatives that there is nothing wrong with the present situation – or that, if there is, it is something which the banks should be left to sort out by themselves – should not be accepted. The suggestion that the present correspondent banking system is inviolable as a way of handling cross-border transfers should also be rejected. From a consumer viewpoint, whatever other merits the correspondent banking system may have, it is conspicuously failing to meet consumers' needs in relation to many cross-border transfers. Given its inherent potential for confusion and delay in cases where the payer's bank and payee's bank do not have accounts with each other, it would appear to be a forlorn task to adapt it to meet the needs of EC consumers in the era of the single market.

At this early stage of discussions, it would appear that some form of linkage of ACHs is the most attractive option from the consumer viewpoint. However, it would be premature to stipulate that this necessarily implies the establishment of a pan-EC clearing house. It would seem to be perfectly feasible for linkage of ACHs to take place under the aegis of an institution which would not itself necessarily get involved in actually operating a clearing house. Such an institution could set or approve standards for technical interfaces between ACHs, establish minimum service levels for member ACHs and supervise arrangements for settlement. It could also act as an accreditation body for existing and new ACHs in terms of their linkage to an EC-wide cross-frontier payment system.

In view of the prudential aspects of the settlement process – and the ever-increasing risk of financial exposure of banks within existing

ACH arrangements – there would be a clear advantage if such an institution was either part of or closely linked to the proposed Eurofed or European System of Central Banks. National central banks should be closely integrated into the supervisory arrangements, given the role they currently play in arrangements for clearing within many member countries. In any event, it is important that the wider public interest (as well as the interests of individual consumers) should be kept firmly to the forefront when satisfactory clearing arrangements for cross-border payments are being planned and implemented, especially to ensure that that there is an effective infrastructure for the development of the single market and that the arrangements are not anti-competitive. The control of such an institution should not therefore be in the hands of the commercial banks, though they would obviously need to be actively involved.

There is not necessarily any conflict between the approach outlined above and the 'market driven' approach which is urged by the banks. The supervisory arrangements need to take full account of the needs of all participants in the market for relatively low value cross-border payments, including consumers and small businesses as well as banks. It should not, though, be assumed that banks are necessarily capable of representing the needs of their customers, or of distinguishing what suits them from what suits their customers.

If the current system does in reality work as well as some banks claim, and the evidence of delays and expense does not reflect the true situation, then the banks should not have any difficulty in demonstrating this. On the other hand, the banks have nothing to lose and much to gain from consumer involvement in any improvements that might be made. If the system can be made to work better for consumers, then the banks will also benefit. It is reassuring that the the Commission has appointed representatives of the interests of individual consumers as members of the Payment Systems Users' Liaison Group, alongside representatives of banking and other interests.

Insurance

It is a paradox that insurance, intended to cushion the consumer against the economic hazards of life (and death), is the most uncertain and problematic of all financial transactions. In exchange for making regular payments, the consumer receives a promise from the insurer. The promise is that at some time in the future, which may or may not be specified, in certain circumstances, defined with varying degrees of precision, the insurer may pay the consumer an amount of money which is usually unpredictable.

Whether the consumer gets paid at all depends on the insurance company staying in business and on how it interprets the provisions of an extremely complex contract which it has itself drawn up. It is virtually impossible for the consumer to know at the time of entering into the contract whether she or he is getting value for money. There may be indicators about value for money – for example, the past performance of an insurance company in relation to with-profits life insurance – but these may or may not prove to be a good guide to what happens in the future. Again, premium rates may or may not be a good guide to value for money – a low premium may prove to be of little benefit if it is offset by ungenerous or delayed treatment of claims.

An additional major complication is that most 'life insurance' is not in fact life insurance at all, but long-term savings. The consumer's premium payments cover both the insurance and savings elements, which are not clearly distinguished. Life insurance is therefore in competition with other long-term forms of savings, such as bank or other deposits, collective investments such as unit trusts and mutual funds, and direct investment in bonds or equities. Increasingly, life insurance is becoming inter-twined with pension provision.

Government Intervention

These are among the reasons why there is a substantial public policy intervention in insurance markets in every member country of the EC. The forms of intervention are many and varied, but include the following:

- Authorisation of entry into the market, which may be general (for example, all life insurance) or specific (for example, separate authorisation for each different type of life insurance business): authorisation may be more difficult for foreign than domestic insurers;
- Continuing prudential controls over size of reserves and financial ratios to ensure that authorised insurers stay in business;
- Procedures for the winding-up of insurers;
- Stipulation of standard insurance contract conditions;
- Limitation on the investment policies of insurers (for example, minimum proportion in domestic investments, maximum proportion in equities);
- Use of standardised mortality tables for life insurance;
- Controls over advertising and selling methods;
- Standardisation or approval of premiums;
- Compulsory insurance requirements (for example, motor liability insurance);
- Actual state provision of insurance either as a monopoly or in competition with private insurers;
- Requirement on life insurers to cede part of their business to a state-owned reinsurer;
- Requirement on government and quasi-government bodies to buy insurance from insurers which are subsidiaries of state-owned banks.

All these forms of government intervention on public policy grounds have the effect of significantly reducing competition. The necessary conditions for a perfectly competitive market do not apply in any EC member country – indeed, it is impossible to envisage perfect competition in insurance. However, the trade-off between competition and regulation is made at widely varying levels in different countries.

Differences in Regulation

Perhaps the most heavily regulated country of all – certainly, in those countries which have sophisticated insurance markets – is Germany (see Finsinger and others 1985 for an excellent short summary of the development of insurance regulation in Germany). Against the experience of frequent failures in the nineteenth century, the Law for Insurance Regulation of 1901 provided a framework for the development of 'orderly markets' and the 'avoidance of destructive competition' – two phrases which should always stimulate scepticism among consumers. It established a persisting tradition of strict regulation, not only over entry to the market but over detailed business operations, premiums, investment practices and contract conditions. Separate authorisation is required for each line of business, each of which must be conducted on the Spartentrennung principle, which involves a legally separate firm being set up for each insurance market – life, health and so on (Moon 1989).

Even for those insurers which succeed in obtaining authorisation, there are significant barriers to competition on price, contract terms and product innovation. Investment policies are controlled – for example, not more than 20 per cent of the assets of life insurers may be held in equities. Insurers are exempted from certain key aspects of Federal Cartel Law.

The Federal Insurance Regulatory Authority, the BAV (Bundesaufsichtsamt für das Versicherungswesen), defends its regime on the grounds that deregulation would harm consumers' interests. However, there is growing criticism on the basis that the regulatory regime is far too 'co-operative', with the main changes being agreed between the BAV and the insurers' trade organisations before implementation (Krakowski 1988). It is said that the whole system has the effect of keeping the least efficient insurer in business, safeguarding excess profits for the rest of the industry.

Pressure for some easing of the regulatory framework in Germany is growing. In representations to the Monopolies Commission, the consumer organisation AgV (Arbeitsgemeinschaft der Verbraucher-verbande) is critical of many of the non-prudential aspects of current regulation, stressing that deregulation should involve a reinterpretation of consumer protection requirements (Schmitz 1989). The Monopolies Commission report advocated extensive deregulation and the Federal Cartel Office (Bundeskartellamt) has been flexing its muscles in relation to the cartel arrangements in the insurance industry. The BAV is even coming under public fire from within its own industry, an unusual event: Deutsche Bank's life insurance subsidiary has criticised it for favouring established insurers against new entrants, in that only insurers that have been established for more than three years can issue a declaration of future dividend bonuses (*Retail Banker International* 27 March 1991). The European Commission's strategy for a single market in insurance services will undoubtedly, in the fullness of time, have a major impact in terms of making the German domestic market more competitive.

Other EC member countries with 'heavy' regulatory regimes for their insurance markets are Greece, Italy and Portugal. Countries which could be described as having 'intermediate' regulation, with varying patterns of control and competition, are Belgium, Denmark, France and Spain – though there are strong political pressures for greater deregulation in Belgium and France, and Spain eased its regulation appreciably in 1984.

The two countries with 'light' regulatory structures are the Netherlands and the UK. Here, regulation focuses mainly on authorisation and on continuing prudential supervision, though the dangers of generalising about regulation are illustrated by the recent tightening up in the UK of controls over advertising and selling methods following the passage of the Financial Services Act 1986.

Some aspects of insurance regulation extend beyond the industry itself to control the actions of the individual consumer. Only in the Netherlands and the UK do consumers have freedom to make an insurance contract with an insurer which is not authorised or established within their own country. There is a blanket prohibition in France, Greece, Ireland and Italy and various partial prohibitions in Belgium, Luxembourg and Germany. The majority of member countries (though not the Netherlands and the UK) also prohibit intermediaries in the consumer's home country from playing a part in effecting such insurance, a form of control which is proving to be one of the many great complications for the European Commission in developing its strategy on life insurance (OECD 1983).

It should be stressed again that light regulatory regimes for an insurance industry do not mean perfect competition. The nature of insurance itself and the way that it is sold ensure that imperfect consumer information is a major obstacle to the impact of competition in the marketplace. For example, even within the competitive and well developed life insurance market in the UK, a comparative survey of 15-year term life insurance contracts for £30,000 (c.21,400 ECU) shows that the premiums payable by a consumer to a typical poor performance insurance company are between 60 and 90 per cent higher than those payable to the best value companies (*Which?* 1986).

When buying – or, rather, being sold – insurance, many consumers are unaware of the savings they might make by comparing premiums, even within the limitations of price as an indicator of value for money in insurance. Another UK study shows that, out of a sample of 2,782 holders of life insurance contracts, only 10 per cent personally examined several contracts before deciding. The same percentage applied to property insurance. Even with home contents insurance, 78 per cent only considered one insurer (Office of Fair Trading 1986).

Market Changes

The insurance market within the Community is growing rapidly – not only absolutely but also relative to the rest of the economy. Insurance premiums within the EC have risen from 4 per cent of Gross Domestic Product in 1970 to 6 per cent in 1988. The European insurance market (all of Europe, not just the EC) is now about three-quarters the size of the US market, and slightly larger than that of Japan (*Sigma* 1990). Life insurance is the fastest growing aspect of insurance – for example, in France, life insurance premiums more than quintupled in the decade between 1978 and 1988, while other forms of savings grew by less than 50 per cent. Increasingly, life insurance is about savings rather than insurance – 'Insurance companies are becoming the main conduit for Europe's savings' (*The Economist* 24 February 1990).

The general picture of growth in the Community's insurance market disguises vast differences in the extent to which individual national markets are developed. In terms of annual premium income for both non-life and life insurance, measured in ECU per head of population, the figures are as follows:

	Annual premium income (ECU per head in 1987)
Germany (West)	1,090
Great Britain	1,016
Netherlands	857
Denmark	790
France	785
Ireland	765
Luxembourg	616
Belgium	534
Spain	316
Italy	293
Germany (East)	203
Portugal	96
Greece	57

(*Sigma* 1990)

This huge variation in premium income per head is only one of the ways in which national insurance markets within the EC are differentiated. Differences in the cost of insurance are another. The BEUC study cited in the earlier chapter on The Grand Design shows a 10:1 ratio between EC countries for similar term life insurance contracts. A study for the Cecchini Report on *The Cost of Non-Europe in Financial Services* shows the following theoretical overall potential for price reductions in a single market for insurance, built up from weighted averages for the life, home, motor, commercial fire and theft, and public liability sectors of the market:

	Estimated theoretical potential price reduction as a result of completing single insurance market
Italy	-51 per cent
Luxembourg	-37
Spain	-32
Belgium	-31
France	-24
Germany	-10
UK	-4
Netherlands	-1

(*Source*: Price Waterhouse 1988)

These figures give some idea of the possible benefit for Community consumers that might stem from the establishment of an internationally competitive single market for insurance throughout the EC.

Acquisitions, Mergers and Joint Ventures

While the achievement of a single European market in insurance is still a long way away, as the rest of this chapter will confirm, the prospective lowering of national barriers has stimulated feverish activity in the financial services industry, in terms of acquisitions, mergers, cross-shareholdings, joint ventures and new start-ups. Some of these structural changes have been domestic and at least partly defensive in intent, such as the 1988 merger of Axa with Compagnie du Midi to form France's second largest insurer and the 34 per cent stake of France's largest insurer, UAP (l'Union des Assurances de Paris) in Groupe Victoire.

A small number of insurers appear to be starting out on the road of building a Community-wide network. For example:

• UAP controls Gesa (Spain) and Royal Belge, has a minority shareholding in Sun Life (UK) and has insurance interests in

Greece, Ireland, Italy and the Netherlands. Through its Groupe Victoire stake it has an interest in Colonia (Germany). UAP, Royal Belge and Sun Life have set up what is claimed to be the first Europe-wide life insurer, PanEurolife *(Retail Banker International* 27 May 1991);

• Generali (Italy) has a minority shareholding in Compagnie du Midi (France), which itself acquired Equity and Law (UK) in 1987;

• Perhaps most significantly of all, Germany's largest insurer, Allianz, acquired Cornhill (UK) in 1986 and has controlling stakes in Italy's second largest insurer, Riunione Adriatica de Sicurita, Ercos (Spain) and the insurance interests of Compagnie de Navigation Mixte (France).

European expansion is not, however, always a path strewn with roses. In January 1991, Guardian Royal Exchange (UK) announced that it was reducing its stake in Italy by selling its two non-life subsidiaries, Cidas and Sipea, acquired as recently as 1989, and by lowering its holding in the life insurer Polaris to 20 per cent *(Retail Banker International* 27 May 1991).

Allfinanz and *Bancassurance*

It is not just the barriers between countries that are being lowered within the insurance industry, but the functional division between insurance and banking. Structural realignments are not limited to the confines of the insurance industry. Within the EC, we are entering the era of *allfinanz* and *bancassurance*, of conglomerates which straddle the different sectors of the financial services industry.

Banks are reported to control 21 major insurance companies in France, nine in Germany and seven in Italy (House of Commons 1989). They appear to be tempted by the apparent profitability of insurance – in 1990, the profits from the insurance operations of Lloyds Bank outstripped profits from its core UK retail banking business *(Euromoney* April 1991). Perhaps the grass always seems to be greener on the other side of the hedge, although the converse acquisition of banks by insurance companies is less marked. There are some examples, however – in France GAN, the third largest state-owned insurer, has bought CIC, a medium sized bank, while in Germany Allianz has taken shareholdings in Bayerische Hypotheken-und-Wechselbank and Bayerische Vereinsbank.

A number of banks are taking a different route by setting up separate life insurance subsidiaries – for example, TSB and Barclays in the UK, Allied Irish Bank in Ireland, Deutsche Bank in Germany and Credit Agricole in France. Royal Bank of Scotland has set up a subsidiary to write motor and property insurance.

Cross-shareholdings between banks and insurance companies are becoming more frequent. In the Netherlands, AMEV, the third largest insurer, and VSB, a savings bank, have cross-shareholdings. In France, Banque Nationale de Paris, the largest bank, and UAP, the largest insurer, have exchanged 10 per cent of their shareholdings, giving them access to each other's distribution networks. Both institutions are publicly owned. A more full-blooded approach is the Netherlands merger between the insurer Nationale-Nederlanden and NMB-Postbank, itself a merger between two major banks.

This merger is reported to have angered Dutch insurance intermediaries, because similar insurance policies will be available more cheaply through banks – premiums of policies sold through banks do not have to take account of the commission paid to intermediaries. This 'dual pricing' of insurance policies – the price depending on the distribution network used – may become increasingly common in future (*Retail Banker International* 11 March 1991).

Increasingly, distribution networks are being considered to be the key to success in financial services markets. The earlier chapter on The Grand Design referred to Allianz's stake in Dresdner Bank and the accompanying agreement that Dresdner Bank would act as an outlet for its insurance business in five länder. Some distribution agreements do not involve any structural link – for example, in the UK Midland Bank and Commercial Union have a joint venture agreement for certain life insurance products, as do Royal Bank of Scotland and Scottish Equitable.

These are only some examples of the current ferment of change in the insurance sector specifically and the financial services industry more generally. It is against this background of market changes and regulatory differences that the European Commission has been following its tortuous pilgrim's path towards a single market for insurance. The rest of this chapter outlines the progress it has made and the possible implications for the consumer.

The Commission's Strategy

Overriding all the detailed complexities of achieving a single market for insurance, there has been a major political difference in perspective which has dominated discussions of the various proposals that have come forward and which has led to a series of awkward compromises. Put simply, the Commission takes the view that an insurer based in any member country has a right, stemming from Article 59 of the Treaty of Rome, to sell in any other member state the types of insurance which it is authorised to sell in its home state. This is a view which has, in the main, been supported by the governments of the Netherlands and the UK.

It has been contested with varying degrees of vigour by the governments of other member countries, headed by Germany. They argue that they have a responsibility to protect their consumers, and that any insurer selling insurance in their countries should be subject to national laws, should be established in the country concerned and should be authorised by the regulatory authority.

At one level, this persisting debate is about the interests of the insurance industries in the countries concerned. We have already seen that regulation is light in the Netherlands and the UK and heavy in Germany. British and Dutch insurers might be expected to gain from the opening up of insurance markets in other EC member countries, while many (though not all) insurers in heavily regulated markets might feel that they have much to lose in more competitive markets.

However, at another level, there is a strong consumer interest in this difference of view. If the rules of competition and regulation are being redrawn in the attempt to create a single market, what is the trade-off for consumers between the possible benefits of greater competition and the possible dilution of consumer protection? This is a question which consumer organisations have been attempting to answer. Not only is the answer difficult to find, but it varies from country to country, because of differences in the existing mix of competition and regulation. It is a question which needs to be kept in the forefront of any consideration of the likely consequence of current Directives and future proposals.

The First Phase

The European Commission's initial strategy was to provide a framework within which insurers authorised in one EC member country could establish branches in other member countries through a system of multiple authorisation. The first step on this road was the adoption in

1973 of the First Non-Life Insurance Directive (73/239/EEC). This provided for a division of responsibilities between the regulatory authorities in the home country where the authorised insurer's head office is situated and in the host country in which it planned to open branches (though the concepts of home and host country had not been formulated as such at the time). It laid down common methods for determining solvency margins and the minimum solvency margin needed as a necessary condition for authorisation by the home country.

A broadly similar First Life Insurance Directive (79/267/EEC) was adopted in 1979. The delay of six years between these two Directives was largely due to the very different approach adopted by member countries to composite insurers – that is, insurers who carry on both life and non-life insurance business. France, Ireland and the Netherlands prohibit composites. Denmark, Germany and Italy have some composites, but do not authorise any new ones. Belgium, Luxembourg and the UK have no restrictions.

Briefly put, the argument against composites is that life insurance funds might be at risk if they are deployed within a composite to meet the insurer's bad experience of non-life risks. The eventual compromise adopted in this Directive was to prohibit new composites, but to allow existing ones to continue in business if that was provided for in the member country's national regulations. However, this approach received something of a setback when Greece, Portugal and Spain subsequently joined the EC, as all three new member countries allow composite insurers (Pool 1990).

The argument about composite insurers is now less intense than it was and there seems to be much wider acceptance of the view that the risks to consumers are negligible. This is manifest in the Commission's proposal for a Third Life Insurance Directive, outlined under The Third Phase below.

Neither of the first phase Directives explicitly provided for freedom of services in insurance – that is, freedom to supply insurance across the Community's internal frontiers. Nor did they deal with non-prudential issues such as advertising and selling methods, general and special policy conditions, and premium or approval. While they codified an important principle, the qualified freedom of establishment, they had little impact in practice on insurance markets.

The Coinsurance Directive (78/473/EEC) of 1978 must also be included in this first phase. While its rules for coinsurance (that is, the participation of several insurers, one of them the lead insurer, in insuring a major risk) are of no direct consequence for consumers, its ambiguity in key respects provided a basis for the Schleicher case and all that has subsequently followed from the judgment of the Court in that case. It was interpreted by some member countries as meaning that the lead insurer must be established in the member country in which the risk was located, against the Commission's view that establishment in any Community country was sufficient.

The Schleicher Case

The Commission took a test case against Germany to the Court of Justice. Essentially, it contested provisions in German legislation which required an insurer covering a risk in Germany to be authorised and established in Germany. Similar cases were taken against Denmark, France and Ireland.

In its judgment, the Court stressed that insurance is a particularly sensitive area so far as policyholder protection is concerned. There might, therefore, in the present state of Community law and in the absence of detailed harmonisation, be imperative public interest reasons which could justify member countries' restrictions on freedom to provide insurance services. Host countries, though not entitled to require insurers to be established in their territory, might nevertheless be justified in imposing their own authorisation procedures. However, any conditions attached to authorisation had to be objectively justified and the host state should not duplicate the home state's regulatory controls.

As one of the exceptions to these general principles, the Court said that controls might be exercised by the host state on policyholder protection grounds. This was further qualified in language whose complexity continues to provide endless scope for legal exegesis, but whose implication seems to be that the need for protection is not necessarily the same in every instance. There may be instances where it is not needed and where separate authorisation would not be justified. However, a high level of host state control may be justified for 'mass risks' because of the individual consumer's difficulty – or that of small business – in making sure that she or he was properly protected and in judging whether the insurer would be able to meet his long-term obligations (Court of Justice 1986).

From the Commission's viewpoint, the Court's judgment settled the point that freedom to supply insurance services stems directly from the Treaty of Rome and does not depend either on prior harmonisation or on establishment in the host country. So far, so good. However, it left the Commission with a monumental headache which has still not been finally cured. The challenge to the Commission has been to find legislative frameworks which will distinguish situations in which buyers of insurance may need 'special protection' – whatever that might consist of – from situations in which such protection is not necessary. The scarcely hidden agenda within this has been how to prevent considerations of special protection being used by some governments to perpetuate existing insular national insurance markets in many countries and to prevent the creation of a genuinely single market.

The Second Phase

The Commission's strategy for dealing with these problems started by defining situations in which, in the context of the Court judgment, special protection is *not* needed. The Second Non-Life Insurance Directive (88/357/EEC) of 22 June 1988 in effect makes a distinction between 'large risks', where insurance is taken out by medium and larger businesses, and 'mass risks', a term of art covering the insurance needs of smaller business and individual consumers. The aim of the Directive is to make it possible for large risks to be insured across frontiers within the Community. This 'freedom of services' has previously only been available in a small minority of countries, including the Netherlands and the UK, and prohibited or seriously circumscribed in most, including France, Germany and Italy.

What is a large risk? The answer depends partly on the nature of the risk and partly on the size of the business of the policyholder whose risk is being insured. All transport risks other than road vehicles are included and all credit and suretyship risks which relate to the policyholder's business. Freedom of services in relation to main property and liability insurance depends on the policyholder's business meeting at least two of the following three criteria:

- Balance sheet total of 12.4 million ECU;
- Net turnover of 24 million ECU;
- 500 employees.

The basic implementation date for the Directive was 1 July 1990, and these thresholds will be halved from 1 January 1993. However, there are lengthy transitional arrangements for Spain, Greece, Ireland and Portugal. Full implementation is not required of Spain until 1

January 1997, and of the other three countries until 1 January 1999. The concept of '1992' as the key to a single European market for insurance is developing considerable elasticity.

Cumul or Non-Cumul?
One significant limitation on freedom of services that survived in a modified form in this Directive relates to the controversial question of 'non-cumul'. This term of art refers to the prohibition in a number of member countries on an insurer which has a branch or branches in the host state from providing insurance services directly from its head office (or branches) in its home state. National host country regulations often require the insurance to be made through the host country branch, which effectively prevents the coverage of multinational risks within a single insurance contract.

The eventual compromise reached in the Second Non-Life Insurance Directive (Article 13) leaves it open to a host country to prohibit freedom of services in relation to classes of insurance which a branch on its territory is authorised to cover, but does not allow other 'non-cumul' restrictions. This is obviously still unsatisfactory in terms of achieving a single market, and has been deleted by the provisions of the subsequent Third Non-Life Insurance Directive (see The Third Phase below).

Host Country Controls
On another key issue, the Directive does not directly confront the desire of a number of member countries to maintain existing national markets rather than create a single insurance market for the whole Community. Member countries shall not be prevented:

> '... from maintaining or introducing laws, regulations or administrative provisions concerning in particular approval of the general and special policy conditions, of forms and other printed documents for use in dealing with policyholders, of scales of premiums and of any other document necessary for the normal exercise of supervision, provided that the rules of the Member State of establishment are not sufficient to achieve the necessary level of protection and the requirements of the member State of the provision of services do not go beyond what is necessary in that respect.' (Article 18)

The effect of this is that it leaves it open to any host member country to require an insurer which wants to provide insurance services, but which is not established, not only to seek an administrative authorisation, but also to comply with all host country rules that do not duplicate the insurer's home country authorisation. It leaves intact existing national regulatory systems and fails to differentiate genuine consumer safeguards in the host country from measures which inhibit domestic and international competition as well as product innovation.

This means that there is still a long road to travel before reaching a single market for insurance. However, despite this and other major deficiencies – of which the most glaring is that it leaves mass risks insurance under host country control – the Second Non-Life Insurance Directive represents a significant move forward by the Commission. It establishes the principle of home country control for freedom of services, if only for large risks. It mortally wounds the non-cumul prohibition and establishes the principle that the policyholder's contract law rules. While it does nothing directly to benefit consumers, it provides a framework for further measures which might do so.

Life Insurance – Active and Passive

The distinction made between large risks and mass risks in the Second Non-Life Insurance Directive could not be used to make progress on the life insurance side. The concept of corporate risk – for example, insuring the property of a large company – cannot be applied to life insurance, where the risk is essentially tied to the life of an individual person.

In order to move at least some way forward, the Commission devised a distinction between the 'active' and 'passive' purchaser of life insurance. In the Second Life Insurance Directive (90/619/EEC) of 8 November 1990, the active consumer is defined as someone who either makes a direct approach to an insurer established in another member country, or makes such an approach through an intermediary established in her or his own country. By taking the first step, such a consumer is deemed not to be in need of the 'special protection' referred to in the Schleicher case judgment. Before making a life insurance contract, the consumer must sign a statement confirming her or his understanding that the insurer is subject to the regulatory controls of the country in which it is established, and not of the consumer's own country (Article 13). The precise form of the statement is laid down in an annex to the Directive.

This limited freedom for the 'active' consumer is simultaneously both safeguarded and qualified by Article 14(5) of the Directive. This prohibits member countries from preventing the consumer from entering into any contract which is lawful in the insurer's country of establishment *unless* it is contrary to public policy in the consumer's member country. This seems to leave a big area of uncertainty surrounding the current legislative ban in some member countries on taking out insurance with an insurer who is not established there.

Insurance sold on a freedom of services basis to 'passive' consumers – the overwhelming majority – may still be subject to national host country regulations which are 'justified on policyholder protection grounds' governing general and special policy conditions, documentation and premiums, to the extent that home country rules are insufficient to achieve the 'necessary level of protection' – which is left undefined.

In most other significant respects – for example, the choice of the applicable contract law – the provisions of the Second Life Insurance Directive are identical to or comparable with those of the previous Second Non-Life Directive.

From the consumer viewpoint, both Second Directives fail to deal with a number of key issues. These include varying national controls (or none) over the investment policies of insurers, harmonisation of minimum consumer protection standards in relation to insurance advertising and selling practices, and the regulation of insurance agents and intermediaries. Another problem area that is specific to life insurance is that some member countries discriminate in their tax treatment of life insurance policies, allowing tax benefits on contracts with domestic insurers, but not on those with foreign insurers.

The Third Phase
Even before the completion of the second phase, the Commission made it clear that it did not intend to back down on attaining its objective of a single European market for insurance:

> 'Simply put, we must achieve for everyone the possibilities which we have either opened up, or are on our way to opening up, for particular groups of consumers. All European citizens should be free to shop where they want for insurance within the single market, and our intention is that companies should be able to operate throughout the Community on the basis of a single insurance licence. Companies will be free, that is, not only to set up branches in other Member States but to sell the full range of their products through freedom of services on the basis of single authorisation and supervision from the country where their head office is located. And they will not have to seek advance authorisation from policies which they sell in another Member State.' (Brittan 1990a)

The conditions necessary to achieve this unambiguous goal are as follows:

• Standardisation of the presentation of insurers' accounts, as a basis for co-ordinating national rules for prudential supervision. One way in which this is being tackled is in the Commission's proposal for a Directive on the annual accounts of insurers (European Commission 1989d). This sets out to establish a common basis for the publication of adequate and comparable information on an insurer's activities and financial position. A measure along these lines is an essential prerequisite for completion of the third and final phase;

• The abolition of national restrictions on cumul;

• The abolition of prior control by national authorities over policy conditions, documentation and premiums;

• The member country where the consumer lives or where the risk is located should govern the choice of contract law.

The Commission's proposal for a Third Non-Life Insurance Directive sets out to meet these conditions. It provides for single authorisation, so that an insurer authorised in one member country will be free to open branches and provide insurance on a freedom of services basis across the EC's internal frontiers without further authorisation. This single passport concept is the same as the one used in the Second Banking Directive and the proposed Investment Services Directive. Initial authorisation and continuing prudential control will be the responsibility of the insurer's home state.

Host countries will no longer have the right to restrict cumul, nor will they be able to require prior approval of premiums or policy conditions. However, host countries will still be able to prohibit the sale of insurance contracts which conflict with their 'legal provisions protecting the general good'.

There will be freedom of choice of contract law for all large risks, but for mass risk contracts (including those entered into by individual consumers) member countries may still require that their own contract law should apply.

Consumers must be told which country supervises the insurer and what arrangements exist for safeguarding the interests of policyholders if the insurer goes bust.

Early in 1991, the Commission published proposals for a Third Life Insurance Directive (European Commission 1991). This is on broadly similar lines to the proposals for a Third Non-Life Directive and is based on the Commission's view that all EC member countries now have an effective system of insurance regulation. It includes proposals for some further co-ordination of national regulatory systems, stopping short of full harmonisation, which is considered by the Commission neither necessary nor feasible. This co-ordination would provide a basis for mutual recognition and the granting of a 'single licence'. Authorisation and supervision of an insurer would become the sole responsibility of the regulatory authorities in the insurer's home state.

The proposed Third Life Directive is aligned with the proposed Third Non-Life Directive in abolishing national restrictions on the prior approval of premium rates and policy conditions and on cumul. Additionally, the Third Life Directive would abolish restrictions on the authorisation and operation of existing and new composite insurers.

The consumer protection measures in the Third Life Directive include the following:

- Clear disclosure to the consumer of the essential elements of the insurance contract she or he is entering into and key changes during the life of the contract;
- An extension to all life insurance policyholders of the cooling-off period of between 14 and 30 days established by the Second Life Directive;
- Continuation of the system set out in the Second Life Directive which generally specifies that the law of the member country of the consumer shall apply, while providing that in certain circumstances the parties may choose the law of another country. No further harmonisation of contract law is proposed;
- Arrangements designed to enable an insurer in one member country to comply with the rules and regulations of another member country in which the insurer wishes to carry on business, including notification of the host country rules which are in the general good;
- Consultation between supervisory authorities in the event of an insurer not complying with relevant legal provisions in the host country and powers to put a stop to any irregularities (Department of Trade and Industry 1991).

From the consumer viewpoint, one of the key requirements in the proposed Third Life Directive is the list (Annex II) of information which the consumer must be given before finalising the contract and during the term of the contract. The list of information which must be given to the consumer before the contract is finalised is as follows:

Information about the insurer

* The name of the company and its legal form;
* The name of the member country in which the head office and where appropriate the agency or branch which issues the policy is situated;
* The address of the head office and, where appropriate, of the agency or branch which issues the policy;

Information about the insurance policy

* Definition of each benefit and each option;
* Term of the policy;
* Means of terminating the contract;
* Means of payment of premiums;
* Means of calculation and distribution of profit participation;
* Indication of surrender and paid-up values, and the extent to which they are guaranteed;
* Information on the premiums for each benefit, both main benefits and supplementary benefits;
* For unit-linked policies, definition of the units to which which the policies are linked;
* Indication of the nature of the underlying assets for unit-linked policies;
* Application of the cooling-off period;
* Indication of the tax arrangements applicable;
* The address of the body or bodies in the member country of the commitment to which any complaints of policyholders, lives assured or beneficiaries of the contract should be addressed.

Information which must be given to the consumer during the term of the contract includes any change in the name, address or legal status of the insurer and, where appropriate, the branch or agency, and any change in policy conditions or relevant law.

If these two third phase proposals are adopted without significant dilution, then the Commission will have attained – or come close to attaining – its objective of establishing the conditions for the development of a single European market for insurance. When – and whether – that single market becomes a reality will depend on the decisions of consumers and insurers.

Which Contract Law Should Apply?

There is one issue of principle which may be of considerable significance to a minority of consumers – the choice of contract law governing an insurance policy. The insurance legislation of the majority of member countries provides for the law of the country where the policyholder lives (or the risk is insured) to govern the contract. For example, in France the applicable law is French law to the exclusion of all others. Only the Netherlands and the UK at present allow the consumer freedom to choose (or, rather, agree with the insurer) which national law rules the contract.

The reasoning behind the restrictive approach is that the consumer might be exploited by her or his inequality of resources and strength compared with the insurer. It has received some support from the consumer quarter:

> 'For a long time, we feared that the Community would promote a free choice of contract law between member states, which would have been a real danger for consumers in the absence of harmonisation ... a policyholder should never find himself in a situation where a contract law is applied with which he has no apparent connection ... [a choice should] always be made by reference to the policyholder's residence or the location of the risks he is insuring'. (Schmitz 1989)

The Second Non-Life Insurance Directive appears to establish the principle that the applicable law is that of the member country in which the insurance commitment is made – 'However, where the law of that State so allows, the parties may choose the law of another country' (Article 7). The principle is then qualified in various complex ways which introduce elements of uncertainty about how it will work out in practice. There are comparable provisions in the Second Life Directive (Article 4).

The principle is somewhat modified in the Third Non-Life Directive, where it is set out as follows:

> 'The Member State in which the risk is situated shall not prevent the policy-holder from concluding a contract conforming with the rules of the home Member State, as long as it does not conflict with legal provisions protecting the general good in the Member State in which the risk is situated.' (Article 25)

There is an identical provision in the proposed Third life Directive (Article 24). While at first sight the modification appears to open up freedom of choice of contract law for the consumer and the insurer, it introduces a major element of uncertainty. As the Commission has not (in this, as in other instances) committed itself to what is or is not in the general good, the whole issue is left to the courts.

The approach to insurance contract law adopted by the Commission has come under scrutiny and has been criticised as not necessarily being in the best interests of consumers. This was the line taken by a number of contributors to the Colloquium on International Insurance Contract Law organised jointly by the University of Innsbruck and the European University Institute at Florence (23 and 24 May 1991). The Commission's approach is seen as being less advantageous to consumers than Articles 3 and 5 of the Rome Convention. There might well be situations in which the consumer would be in a better position if the insurance contract was governed by the law of the insurer's country than by her or his own national law. Also, the existing provisions in the Directives are criticised for introducing an undesirable discrepancy between banking and insurance law.

It might be possible to resolve this highly specific but complex issue in the context of a wider harmonisation of insurance contract law within the Community. However, the Commission's early initiative, dating back to 1979, to introduce a proposed Directive on this seems to have come to a halt.

Motor Insurance
The Commission's efforts in relation to motor insurance have taken a different path, mainly because each member country has developed different systems for civil liability. Through the First Motor Insurance Directive (72/166/EEC) of 24 April 1972, the Second Motor Insurance Directive (84/5/EEC) of 30 December 1983 and the Third Motor Insurance Directive (90/232/EEC) of 14 May 1990, the Community has developed a system of legislation on compulsory motor insurance which is harmonised to a considerable degree. The main characteristics of this from the consumer viewpoint are as follows:

- Motor liability insurance is compulsory in each member country;
- A policy issued in any member country must be valid in all other member countries;
- A policy must cover liability for personal injuries and property damage, above certain minimum levels of cover;
- National guarantee funds must provide compensation at at least these minimum levels for injury or damage caused by uninsured drivers;

- National guarantee funds are prohibited from requiring victims of uninsured drivers to establish that the person liable is unable or refuses to pay;
- Compensation to victims should not be delayed by disputes between the guarantee fund and a civil liability insurer as to who is liable to pay;
- Those involved in a road accident must be able to identify the insurers of the vehicle involved.

As motor liability insurance is outwith the scope of the Second Non-Life Insurance Directive, the Commission needed to make sure that progress was made in establishing freedom of services in relation to motor insurance. The Motor Services Insurance Directive (90/618/EEC) of 8 November 1990 does just that. Because it maintains the same distinction between large risks and mass risks, it is of little direct and immediate consequence to the individual consumer as a purchaser of insurance, rather than as victim of a road accident.

The Consumer Agenda

After a long and arduous journey, the Commission may well feel that the end of the road on insurance is just over the horizon. Simultaneously aided and thwarted by the Court's Schleicher case judgment, it has used considerable ingenuity in pushing onwards, often against the determined opposition of some member countries.

From the consumer viewpoint, there must still be mixed feelings. At times, it has seemed as though the Commission has been grossly neglecting the interests of the individual consumer in order to further the interests of large business – an impression compounded by the failure, until relatively recently, of both the Commission and most national governments to consult consumer interests.

On the credit side of the balance sheet, existing and proposed Directives will in due course abolish many national regulations which have stifled competition and innovation, and served to maintain unnecessarily high insurance premiums. Prior approval of general and special contract conditions, premium fixing or approval by regulatory authorities, the prohibition on cumul, and restrictions on the freedom of insurers established in other member countries will all go.

No Harmonisation of Consumer Protection

On the debit side, there is as yet no minimum harmonisation of consumer protection. Host countries may retain or introduce consumer protection measures if they are in 'the general good', but this concept almost certainly creates more problems than it solves, as the general good is not defined, even in outline. It is presumably left to the Court to decide.

Inadequate Compensation Provisions

The position of consumers who have contracts with an insurer which goes bankrupt is still uncertain. In the UK, there are statutory arrangements under the Policyholders' Protection Act to compensate consumers in such circumstances. In most other member countries, reliance is currently placed on authorisation and supervision procedures to prevent insurers from going bankrupt, but the impact of Community measures on national regulatory systems means that it will no longer be possible to rule out bankruptcy.

The Commission's proposal for a Directive on Compulsory Winding-Up of Insurance Undertakings (European Commission 1989b) is intended to establish EC-wide procedures for the compulsory winding-up (as distinct from the voluntary liquidation) of insurers. It includes provisions for a harmonised preferential treatment for insurance creditors. However, this leaves two gaps:

- The transitional arrangements before the Directive is adopted. At present, there are wide variations between member countries. Aside from the UK's compensation fund, some countries require insurers to establish a separate fund out of which claims are paid in the event of insolvency, while others give preferential treatment to policyholders and third parties relative to other creditors;
- Even when the Directive is adopted, there will still not be either a Community-wide compensation fund or a system of harmonised national compensation funds.

At the time of writing, the effective compensation of consumers in the event of an insurer's insolvency is a notable gap in the Commission's measures.

Consumer Complaints and Redress

Denmark, the Netherlands and the UK all have relatively informal schemes for the independent resolution of consumer complaints about insurers. Although very different in their structure and method of operation, all three schemes provide a fast, effective and cheap way of handling consumer complaints and providing redress where it is justified. They operate outside the formal legal system but do not take away consumers' legal rights (Wiesner 1990).

These three schemes do not at present handle cross-border complaints, nor are there similar schemes in other member countries. As one of the Commission's aims is to promote the provision of insurance on a cross-border freedom of services basis, from the consumer viewpoint it would seem to be a natural corollary that there should be a Community-wide system for dealing with complaints.

Agents and Intermediaries

Broadly speaking there are three different ways in which insurance is sold:

- Directly, by the insurer's own sales force (les salariés des enterprises);
- By agents appointed by the insurer (les agents généraux);
- By independent intermediaries or brokers (les courtiers).

The relative importance of these three sales or distribution networks varies very considerably between member countries. For example, some countries have no independent intermediaries. The regulation of agents and independent intermediaries also varies from the intensive to the non-existent. In the Netherlands, independent intermediaries are regulated under the Insurance Intermediaries Act 1952, and their registration with the Social-Economic Council is subject to passing examinations. In France, the Code of Insurance lays down professional requirements for intermediaries. In the UK, insurers' representatives and appointed agents are regulated under the Financial Services Act 1986 by the Life Assurance and Unit Trust Regulatory Organisation (LAUTRO), while independent intermediaries are regulated by the Financial Intermediaries, Managers and Brokers Regulatory Association (FIMBRA).

Intermediaries can – and frequently do – play a critical role in providing the information which guides or determines consumers' choice of insurance. Consumers may rely on intermediaries for guidance about the most suitable kind of insurance to meet their needs, value for money and choice of insurer. Indeed, the size and diversity of insurance markets often means that it is impracticable for consumers to search the market for themselves. The role that intermediaries play in ensuring that consumers make sensible choices could be considerably enhanced by the development of a Community-wide market.

It is therefore unfortunate that most discussion of the role that intermediaries could play is focused on the large risks market, where large businesses are well placed to ensure that they get good value for money. For individual consumers, the use of appointed agents and independent intermediaries presents problems. The European Consumer Law Group (1986) has pointed to the need for a requirement for intermediaries to disclose their commission payments and this issue is currently the subject of considerable debate in the UK. Other issues that have been identified in Belgium, France, and elsewhere include:

• Consumer confusion about whether an intermediary is working for one company, several companies, or is truly independent;
• Lack of clarity about the legal obligations of intermediaries to consumers;
• Lack of professional qualifications and training;
• Unprofessional selling techniques that are sometimes used.
(Rapport Cortesse 1985: Maystadt 1985: Schmitz 1988)

The OECD Consumer Policy Committee has come out with a set of recommendations about intermediaries:

• Licensing or regulation of intermediaries based on professional qualifications or other proofs of competence;
• Professional training and education requirements;
• The creation of voluntary codes of conduct for selling practices;
• The enforcement of sanctions for unfair selling practices;
• The liability of insurance companies for the negligence, misrepresentation or fraudulent acts of their agents and employees;
• Provisions concerning abusive 'twisting' – advising the purchase of a replacement policy counter to the consumer's best interest;
• Clear disclosure to the consumer of the intermediary's self interest in the transaction;
• The provision to consumers throughout the life of the policy of information concerning the current cash value of all profits allocated to the policy (OECD 1987).

This OECD list is a good consumer agenda of issues raised by the use of insurance agents and intermediaries. It is a long way from being dealt with by the Commission. The early Insurance Intermediaries Directive (77/92/EEC) of 13 December 1976 is intended to provide for the freedom of establishment of intermediaries and their freedom to provide services. It specifies the levels of training and experience for particular activities and requires member countries to accept evidence that intermediaries who have met these levels in another EC country as being sufficient to meet their own national requirements.

However, there are serious doubts as to whether this Directive has been effectively implemented in a number of member countries. In any event its provisions do not go far enough to sustain the structure for freedom of services in insurance envisaged by the second and third phase Directives, never mind minimum consumer protection needs. It is clear that the Commission has important unfinished – indeed, scarcely started – business in relation to intermediaries and agents, summed up by the former Head of Insurance Division in DG XV of the Commission:

> 'If the common market in insurance is to work properly, it is not sufficient to think merely in terms of freedom for brokers and agents to establish in the different Member States and to provide cross-frontier services. There must be the same high level of confidence in intermediaries throughout the length and breadth of the Community and there must, broadly speaking, be the same understanding of what a broker is and does and what an agent is and does. This in turn involves an appreciation of standards that must be accepted by brokers and agents in order to ensure the good image and public acceptance of their professions.' (Pool 1980)

Saving and Investing

Consumers in different Community countries vary considerably in their approach to savings and investment. Savings ratios – that is, savings as a proportion of net disposable income – vary widely:

- EC countries with high savings ratios (averaging at least 15 per cent between 1974 and 1986) include Italy, Greece, France and Belgium;
- Those with medium savings ratios (averaging 12–13 per cent over the same period) include the Netherlands and Germany;
- Spain and the UK are among those with low savings ratios (averaging under 9 per cent).

These savings ratios change over time, and tended to fall in most countries throughout most of the 1980s until around 1987 (earlier in Germany) when they started to rise. However, the differences between countries are quite stable and suggest distinctive national attitudes to saving.

There are also big differences in the ways in which consumers save. The savings component of life insurance is high in the UK and Ireland, virtually unknown in Greece, Spain and Portugal. The popularity of building society accounts in the UK and Ireland is not confined to those saving to buy their first home: there are four times as many building society savers as mortgage holders and some 55 per cent of building society savings are held by people aged 55 or over (Council of Mortgage Lenders 1990). Individual consumers in Belgium, France, Germany and the Netherlands are much more interested in investing in fixed interest bonds than in equities: even indirect investment in equities through equity-based unit trusts and similar funds still seems to have relatively little appeal in continental Europe, though the tide may be beginning to turn.

It is of course always difficult to judge whether differences of this kind are due to fundamental differences in the attitudes of consumers or to variations in the kinds of savings 'products' on offer. What can be said with some confidence is that, within the EC, the interaction of demand for and supply of savings has produced a wide array of varying legal and regulatory frameworks and contrasting methods by which savings products are bought and sold. This chapter deals with the Commission's attempts to deal with this diversity in relation to unit trusts and similar funds, and to investment services more generally.

UCITS – Unit Trusts and Similar Funds

This variability was one of the reasons which accounted for the very long negotiations that took place in preparing a Directive covering UCITS, the acronym for Undertakings for Collective Investment in Transferable Securities. (This is a term of art developed within the EC which covers what are known as Unit Trusts in the UK and Ireland – roughly equivalent to Anlagefonds in Germany, Fonds Commun de Placement in Belgium, France and Luxembourg, and Mutual Funds in the US – as well as Open-ended Investment Companies – Investitionsgesellschaft in Germany, and Sociétés d'Investissement à Capital Variable and Sociétés d'Investissement à Capital Fixe in Belgium, France and Luxembourg). Discussions first began in 1968, but it was not until 20 December 1985 that the UCITS Directive (85/611/EEC) was finally adopted. The implementation date for the Directive was 1 October 1989, with postponements for Greece and Portugal until 1 April 1992. There is a parallel Directive which deals with liberalisation of cross-border transactions in units, with the same implementation date of 1 October 1989, except that Portugal was allowed until 31 December 1990. In the UK, the UCITS Directive has been implemented by Chapter VIII of the Financial Services Act 1986 and various regulations made under it, such as the Authorised Unit Trust Scheme (Investment and Borrowing Powers) Regulations 1988.

The UCITS Directive is something of a hybrid of the Commission's 'old' and 'new' approaches to building a single market for financial services. It contains a number of detailed harmonisation provisions which are not found in more recent framework directives on banking and insurance, but it is nevertheless founded on the 'passport' principle that a UCITS which is properly authorised in one member country may be sold in others without separate authorisation.

The main criteria which determine whether or not a unit trust or similar fund falls within the definition of a UCITS are:

* At least 90 per cent of the capital raised must be invested in quoted securities;
* The risk must be spread, with normally not more than 5 per cent invested in quoted securities of the same company;
* Capital must be raised by means of offers open to the public;
* Unitholders must be able to redeem or repurchase units on request;
* It must be based in an EC country.

These criteria effectively rule out a number of unit trusts and similar funds from being classified as UCITS, including the following:

* Money market and currency funds;
* Property-based funds;
* Investment clubs with restricted membership;
* Investment trusts which have quoted shares;
* Closed-ended funds;
* Funds based on 'derivative instruments' such as futures and options;
* Funds such as Exempted Unit Trusts (UK), Fonds d'Intéressement (France) and Spezialfonds (Germany) which make offers that are limited to certain categories of investors, such as insurance funds and pension funds;
* Funds based outside the EC, for example in Switzerland or the US, even though they meet other UCITS criteria.

A unit trust or similar fund which does not meet the criteria set out in the UCITS Directive is not of course prohibited. It can operate domestically within whatever set of national rules applies in the country in which it is based. However, it does not carry the 'passport' conferred by UCITS status, of not requiring separate authorisation in whatever Community country its units are marketed. While it is open to a member state to impose requirements stricter than those laid down in the Directive to UCITS established in its own country, it cannot generally do so in relation to an 'incoming' UCITS authorised in another EC member state.

The Directive contains a number of provisions dealing with the authorisation, supervision, structure and management (including investing and borrowing practices) of UCITS, all designed to ensure a measure of harmonisation, especially in relation to prudential supervision. A number of these have an element of consumer protection, but there are other provisions which bear directly on consumer information. Each UCITS has to publish a prospectus, annual report and half-yearly report, and the minimum information which these documents must include is set out in two annexes to the Directive.

A key consumer protection provision is the one that leaves control of the marketing and selling of the units of a UCITS in the hands of the 'host' country. This is not evident at first sight, but is implicit in the wording of Article 44 (1):

> 'A UCITS which markets its units in another Member State must comply with the laws, regulations and administrative provisions in that State which do not fall within the field governed by this Directive.'

As marketing and selling are not covered by the Directive, this means that they remain under host country control. However, when applying its laws and regulations about marketing and selling, the host country must not discriminate against UCITS based in another member country. The same rules must apply to both.

The original proposal for a Directive required a UCITS to 'comply with the marketing rules' of any member state in which its units were marketed, including rules on promotion, unfair competition, and direct selling or other methods of marketing. During the protracted discussions, this approach was dropped as it was thought that the expression 'marketing rules' was vague and ambiguous. The convoluted wording of Article 44(1) quoted above was the best that could be devised, but it is in fact very significant for consumers. For example, some countries forbid the doorstep selling of units, or selling units 'off the page' from advertisements in newspapers. They will be allowed to retain this prohibition even if the country in which a particular UCITS is established permits such selling methods on its own territory – providing the prohibition is not discriminatory (European Commission 1988d).

The Consumer Agenda
The UCITS Directive provides a framework within which units in funds which qualify as UCITS may be sold throughout the EC. As well as the indirect protection that it gives to consumers through the standards it lays down for authorisation and management, it does not

erode existing national regulations which control the marketing and selling of units. In this it offers consumers a better deal than the later and wider-ranging Second Banking Directive.

In theory, consumers should have a wider choice of unit trusts and similar funds, as UCITS based in other EC countries may now be available. However, there are a number of practical difficulties which look as if they will constrain the development of an EC-wide market in UCITS, including the following:

- There are differences in the way that units are priced. Most UK units have two prices at any one time, a higher price at which the consumer may buy ('offer price') and a lower price at which the consumer may redeem her or his units ('bid price'). In most other countries units have a single price, with a charge levied on sale or redemption. Consumers may find it difficult to get used to different pricing practices.

- There are variations in tax treatment from country to country. For example, in the UK the fund is taxed and dividends are paid net of tax, while in most other countries dividends and interest are paid gross and any tax liability rests with the individual consumer. There are also differences in the tax treatment of capital gains. Adverse tax treatment makes UK-based UCITS relatively unattractive to consumers in other EC countries and has even prompted some UK management companies to base their funds in Luxembourg, the first EC country to align its domestic legislation with the UCITS Directive, and which also has a UCITS-friendly tax regime (Elvinger 1988).

- There are major differences in the distribution channels between countries and in the ways that units are marketed and sold. In most EC countries UCITS management companies are subsidiaries of banks and insurance companies, which act as a distribution channel for units to 'captive' consumers who already have a strong relationship with the bank or insurance company concerned. In the UK, unit trusts launched by commercial banks and insurance companies have to compete with unit trusts run by merchant banks, stockbrokers and specialised unit trust management companies. Also, independent intermediaries play a significant part in selling units in the UK and Ireland, but are either weak or unknown in other EC countries. The highly diversified market in the UK can be contrasted with Germany, where funds linked to Deutsche Bank, Dresdner Bank and

Commerzbank have 65 per cent of the market. The market in France is also relatively concentrated – Crédit Agricole, Banque Nationale de Paris and Caisse des Dépôts et Consignations share 39 per cent of the business *(The Economist* 29 April 1989).

With the emphasis on distribution, there has been a certain amount of early skirmishing through acquisitions and networking agreements. Dresdner Bank have bought Thornton (UK) and Societé Générale (France) have bought Touche Remnant (UK). Wardley, the UK funds management branch of Hongkong and Shanghai Bank, have a collaborative agreement with Crédit du Nord (France) and a subsidiary of Banca Nazionale del Lavoro (Italy), while Hambros (UK) are working with Istituto Bancario San Paolo di Torino (Italy) and Banco Bilbao Vizcaya (Spain). It remains to be seen whether any of these arrangements has more than a marginal effect on consumer choice and whether any truly pan-Community UCITS will emerge. So far, the most notable example is Robeco (Netherlands), whose operation is so substantial that the provisions of the UCITS Directive had to be stretched at some points to make sure that it was included.

Investment Services
Widely differing legal and regulatory frameworks have also contributed to the slow progress that is being made in formulating a Directive on investment services. After going through several drafts, the Commission produced a proposal on 3 January 1989 (European Commission 1989a) and an amended proposal on 23 January 1990 (European Commission 1990b). The explanation and comments below refer to the revised text issued on 28 May 1990, which will be subject to further changes before it is finally adopted.

The proposed Directive is an ambitious attempt to deal not only with the different regulatory frameworks in EC member countries, but also with the varied nature of securities markets and investment firms. It covers any investment firm carrying out one or more of a defined range of investment *services* in relation to a specified list of *financial instruments*. The range of investment services is:

- Arranging and executing orders;
- Dealing as principal;
- Market-making;
- Portfolio management;
- Underwriting.

The list of financial instruments is:

• Transferable securities;
• Units of a collective investment undertaking;
• Money market instruments;
• Financial futures;
• Options.

Any investment firm authorised to carry out any of these core services would without separate authorisation be allowed to carry out what the proposed Directive calls 'ancillary services', defined as follows:

• Arranging or entering into contracts relating to interest rates or interest rate and/or exchange rate swaps;
• Investment advice;
• Safekeeping and administration of financial instruments;
• Foreign exchange transactions.

The overall approach of the proposed Directive is closely aligned with that of the Second Banking Directive, in that once an investment firm is authorised in its 'home' state, it then requires no further authorisation to set up branches or provide services on a cross-border basis in other 'host' countries of the Community. However, if an investment firm based in EC country 'A' sets up a subsidiary in another EC country, 'B', then the subsidiary's home state is 'B'.

The proposed Directive sets out the minimum requirements which must be used by regulators in member countries in home state authorisation of investment firms. These include:

• Minimum capital requirements which will be laid down in a separate Capital Adequacy Directive. The Commission's proposal for this is currently under discussion;
• People who run an investment firm must be 'of sufficiently good repute and experience';
• The regulator must be satisfied as to the 'suitability' of those holding 10 per cent or more of the capital or voting rights of an investment firm;
• The investment firm must submit a business plan setting out its types of business and organisational structure.

Member countries must also have minimum 'prudential' rules enforced on a continuing basis by the home state regulatory authorities. These cover:

- Administrative, accounting and internal control procedures;
- Protection of investors' ownership rights in their securities;
- Protection of investors' money;
- Either membership of the investment services firm in a general compensation scheme which safeguards investors in the event of bankruptcy or default, or equivalent individual arrangements;
- The right of the regulator to require information from the investment services firm;
- The right of the regulator to require the investment services firm to keep records;
- The need for the investment firm ' ... to be structured and organised in such a way as to minimise the risk of clients' interests being prejudiced by conflicts of interest between the firm and its clients or between one of its clients and another.'

If an authorised investment services firm wants to open branches or provide services in another Community country, it must notify its home regulator and provide certain information, which the home regulator then passes on to the host country regulator. However, the information requirements for opening branches are greater than those for merely providing services.

Early drafts of the proposed Directive required member states to draw up conduct of business rules in accordance with general criteria set out in the text. It was intended that these should provide for investment services firms to take account of the investor's individual circumstances, warn of any risks involved, and give advice which was neutral and in the investor's best interest. This minimal harmonisation of consumer protection provisions has now disappeared. It is left to each member country to apply such conduct of business rules as it has – although of course on a non-discriminatory basis as between firms for which it is the home state and those for which it is host. Indeed this applies to all ' ... legal rules and regulations ... adopted in the interest of the general good' which fall outside the limits of the proposed Directive. The proposed Directive sets out the procedures to be taken by the host country regulator in carrying out enforcement action against an investment services firm authorised elsewhere.

Consumer Issues
It looks as if the building of a single market for investment services will present consumers (as investors in this instance) with the familiar and

uncertain trade-off between wider choice – possibly accompanied by more competition in some countries – and the dilution of existing national consumer protection measures. The key issues are the division of powers between home and host country regulators, compensation schemes, complaints and redress and conflict of interest. The content of the proposed Capital Adequacy Directive, which is linked to the Investment Services Directive, and the timing of the implementation of these Directives, also gives rise to problems.

Home and Host Country Regulation

Existing national laws and regulations are not directly threatened by the proposed Directive. However, in relation to laws and regulations which have been made to implement the proposed Directive, prodigious difficulties might face a host regulator in trying to enforce them against a transgressing firm authorised elsewhere which is providing investment services through branches or across borders. The host country regulator will not be able to withdraw authorisation, but must normally go through an elaborate information and consultative procedure with the home country regulator as a basis for action by the home country regulator.

This may well give rise to the extraordinary situation that the regulator in country A (the home country) is supposed to take legal or other enforcement action against an investment firm which it has itself authorised for offences alleged to have been committed in country B (host country), which, while contrary to the laws or regulations of B, may be legal in A. There is sufficient latitude in the drafting of the proposed Directive for this to happen: many of the requirements stipulated are minimum ones, and some countries may well wish to set higher standards in their implementing legislation. It is difficult to envisage home country regulators pursuing vigorous enforcement practices in such circumstances.

On the plus side, the proposed Directive does allow the host country regulator to take enforcement action against an incoming investment services firm which infringes those of its conduct of business rules which have been 'adopted in the interest of the general good'. This is a familiar concept in the Commission's initiatives to create a single market. It is well-intentioned in that it is designed to prevent member countries from introducing or retaining protection measures in the guise of consumer protection, but it will almost certainly mean that regulator's actions are subject to legal challenges in the courts.

The proposed Directive also allows the host country regulator, in emergencies, to '... take any precautionary measures necessary to protect the interests of investors and others to whom services are provided'. However, this procedure is only a prelude to the normal consultative procedure and eventual home country enforcement – and even this interim power that rests with the host country regulator can be countermanded by the Commission.

The danger to the system as a whole is that some 'incoming' investment services firms operating from branches or on a services only basis will be prepared to take risks in breaking host country rules, knowing that they will have a fair chance of getting away with it. This could well give rise to a general downward pressure to lower regulatory standards.

Investor Compensation Schemes

A second weakness in the proposed Directive is its failure to deal adequately with compensation schemes, to make sure that, if an investment services firm defaults or goes bust, investors are properly compensated. The current situation in the EC is that some member countries have well-developed compensation arrangements, while others do not. The proposed Directive does not establish any minimum standards for compensation schemes – for example, whether a claim is payable in full, and up to what ceiling. As worded, the proposed Directive seems to suggest that compensation schemes are a matter for home state regulators, although it is understood that the Commission are minded to change this so that branches in a host member state would be subject to the host country compensation scheme, while business done on a services only basis would be subject to the home country compensation scheme. An investment services firm would be required to disclose to investors which compensation scheme applies.

This is a completely unsatisfactory situation from the consumer viewpoint. It would mean that compensation would depend quite arbitrarily on the way in which business is done, with the consumer having to compare the merits of up to 12 different compensation schemes, one for each EC member country. It should be a matter of urgency for the Commission to ensure that, before it is adopted, the proposed Directive should include adequate minimum requirements for compensation schemes.

Complaints and Redress

Schemes for dealing rapidly, cheaply and effectively with consumers' complaints – and providing redress where justified – have developed in some EC countries, including Denmark, the Netherlands and the UK. Indeed, in the UK it is a statutory requirement that for a self-regulatory organisation (SRO) to be recognised it ' ... must have effective arrangements for the investigation of complaints against the organisation or its members' (Financial Services Act 1986). In the UK there is now a rather confusing plethora of financial services industry based complaints and redress schemes, some of which – for example, the Investment Referee scheme used by the Financial Intermediaries, Brokers and Managers Regulatory Association (FIMBRA) – involve investment services firms.

However, the existing schemes do not seem to be competent to deal with complaints about a foreign investment services firm which is authorised in another country. This issue is not dealt with in the proposed Directive. It is a problem which affects all financial services, not just investment services firms, and it is referred to again in the concluding chapter.

Conflicts of Interest

A further weakness – from the consumer viewpoint – in the proposed Directive is the vague and general character of its reference to possible conflicts of interest, which is quoted above. While the proper organisation and structuring of an investment services firm may help, they are unlikely to be enough in themselves to safeguard consumers against a conflict of interest. Requirements about disclosure and best execution may be needed to reduce the effects of conflict of interest to an acceptable level, but the host country regulator is powerless to enforce these as they are the responsibility of the home country regulator (Department of Trade and Industry 1990a).

Again, the home country regulator is unlikely to be enthusiastic about enforcing provisions which apply in the host state but which are not part of the regulatory apparatus in the home state itself. This is a further example of the danger that incoming investment services firms from member countries with weak consumer protection regimes will tend to undermine stronger national consumer protection systems.

Capital Adequacy of Investment Services Firms

The Commission's proposal for a Directive setting out the minimum capital requirements for investment firms is an essential complement to both the draft Investment Services Directive and the Second Banking Directive (European Commission 1990g). Its aim is to co-ordinate rules on authorisation and ongoing supervision of investment firms as a necessary basis for the single licence approach – and in particular to make sure that there is a level playing field between non-bank investment firms and credit institutions trading in securities markets.

The proposal sets out minimum initial capital requirements for investment firms which are not credit institutions. Capital requirements for the latter are set by the Second Banking Directive and are at a higher level, despite the level playing field criterion, the justification for this being that banks and other credit institutions engage in a much wider range of activities than specialised investment firms. However, the proposal's capital requirement in relation to both foreign exchange risk and investment business applies to both investment firms and credit institutions.

From the consumer viewpoint, the most controversial aspect of the proposal concerns the initial capital requirements for investment firms. This is set at three levels:

- 500,000 ECU (c.£345,000) as a general requirement, with member countries having the power if they wish to reduce this to the two lower levels below;
- 100,000 ECU (c.£69,000) where a firm holds client money or securities when dealing as agent or acting as portfolio manager, but not itself taking trading positions;
- 50,000 ECU (c.£34,500) where a firm is not authorised to hold client money or securities, or to act as market maker or underwriter, except where the firm distributes issues only on a best efforts basis.

Firms which only provide investment advice will not have to meet initial capital requirements, but otherwise all investment firms will have to do so, whether or not they operate outside their own national borders.

The UK Consumers in the European Community Group (CECG) is concerned that the present proposals are likely to bear heavily on independent financial advisers. While the proposal includes a heavily qualified 'grandfathering' provision which exempts investment firms in existence at the time the Directive is implemented, CECG considers that the Directive as at present drafted will lead to a shrinkage in the number of independent financial advisers, because it raises barriers to new entrants in the domestic as well as the Community-wide market. Also, the grandfathering provision no longer applies when a firm changes hands (other than through inheritance). CECG makes the point that ' ... a choice of distribution channels for financial services is advantageous to consumers – both in terms of offering them a range of different services from which to choose the one that suits them best, and in stimulating competition between those different channels' (Consumers in the European Community Group 1990b).

CECG's approach is to urge that the exemption for firms which only offer investment advice should be extended to those intermediaries which also arrange the execution of orders for buying or selling securities, but which are not authorised to hold client money. This is the initial view taken by the UK government (Department of Trade and Industry 1990c). At the time of writing, it is not clear what the response of other member countries and of the Commission itself will be to this view. It is likely to come up against the familiar problem of variations in industry structure between member countries – the concept of independent investment intermediaries is virtually unknown in some EC countries.

Implementation Date

There is a particular problem about the implementation date of the proposed Investment Services Directive and associated Capital Adequacy Directive. The Second Banking Directive, which has already been adopted, must be implemented by member countries by 1 January 1993. This will allow authorised 'credit institutions' (including banks) which provide investment services to do so throughout the EC on the basis of their home country 'passports'. If the Investment Services Directive has a later implementation date, then there will be a marked competitive inequality which will favour banks at the expense of investment services firms.

There are major structural differences between member countries in the way that investment services are marketed – for example, in Germany the banks are overwhelmingly dominant, while in the UK independent intermediaries have a significant market share. If the implementation dates are not aligned, it would mean, for example, that German and other EC banks would be able to operate freely in the investment services market in the UK, but UK investment services firms would not have the freedom given by the Investment Services Directive to operate in the German and other EC member country markets. From the point of competitive equality, it is therefore of some importance that the Second Banking Directive and the Investment Services Directive should be implemented simultaneously.

Progress is slow. The UK and some other governments are adhering to the main thrust of the Commission's proposal that, once an intermediary is authorised in one member country, it should be free to offer investment services in other Community countries without separate authorisation or establishment. The French government maintains that certain investment transactions should be reserved for regulated stock exchanges. There are also disputes about the access of banks to regulated stock exchanges and about the speed with which trades should be reported – a transparency issue (*Amex Bank Review* 3 April 1991).

At the time of writing, there appear to be differences in the philosophy of regulating securities markets, as well as varied views on significant detail, which are proving to be major obstacles to the forward movement of the propoposal.

Private Pensions

Many consumers spend a significant part of their income in saving or investing for retirement. Broadlly speaking, there are three ways of doing this – through state social security schemes, through occupational or professional pension schemes, and through private arrangements (for example, life insurance policies, investments in unit trusts, bonds or other securities, and personal pension arrangements). The European Commission has started to consider the single market implications of retirement provision and has issued a working paper on this extremely complex subject (European Commission 1990j).

At this stage, the Commission is focusing its attention on occupational and professional pension schemes. Some aspects are already subject to Community Directives or Commission proposals dealt with elsewhere in this report under banking, life insurance and investment services. However, there remains a big gap. The Commission argues that the economic importance of pension funds to the effective operation of the single market for financial services is considerable. It estimates that the assets of EC pension funds (excluding the pension assets of insurers) amounted to 700 billion ECU at 31 December 1989 and says that the Capital Liberalisation Directive would lose some of its impact if EC-based pension funds did not have the freedom to make the best investment decisions on a Community-wide basis.

At present, a number of EC countries impose restrictions on pension funds' freedom to invest. Portugese and Danish funds are not allowed to invest abroad. Italian funds cannot hold more than 20 per cent of their money in private companies. In France, pension funds must hold a minimum of 34 per cent of assets in state bonds and not more than 5 per cent in shares in foreign insurers. German funds cannot hold more than 5 per cent of assets in foreign bonds. Belgian funds must put 15 per cent of their technical reserves into Belgian government bonds. There are also restrictions on management – Portugal and Spain exclude foreign firms (European Commission 1990j: *The Economist* 30 March 1991).

A further reason for tackling the occupational and professional pensions area is that multi-national employers are often faced with the inefficient and inequitable reality of having to set up separate national pension schemes in each of the countries in which they operate. Also, employees moving from one country to another may have to leave their employer's pension scheme in one country and join a different scheme in another country, even while remaining in the same employment. The Commission therefore proposes to tackle the problems covering managed and self-administered pension funds which are not already covered by provisions in Community Directives and Commission proposals on banking, life insurance and investment services.

The Commission has it in mind to pursue a three-pronged approach on the following lines:

- Freedom of cross-border pension fund management. The intention here is that any pension fund manager established and authorised in one member country should be able to operate in all EC countries on the basis of this authorisation – the now familiar 'single passport' approach;
- Freedom of cross-border investment for pension funds. At present, a number of member countries have constraints on investment which do not seem to be justifiable solely on prudential grounds;
- Freedom of cross-border membership of pension funds. The Commission's intention is to ensure that pension funds are free to accept members resident in other EC countries and that, correspondingly, residents of each EC country are free to become members of a non-domestic pension fund.

At the time of writing, no formal proposals have yet been put forward, but it is already clear that the Commission's first two objectives are easier to achieve than the third, the one which is of most direct interest to consumers. The Commission stresses that to attain its goal of cross-border membership it is not necessary to harmonise benefit levels or structures, especially in view of the wide differences there are in social security retirement provisions between member countries. However, it believes it is necessary:

- To create a co-ordinated basis for mutual recognition of regulatory systems and home country control;
- To develop a framework for taxation which ensures that tax dispensations are not abused but which does not impede cross-border memebrship;
- To remove all direct and indirect restrictions in national laws which reduce the practicability of cross-border membership.

These are considerable obstacles which have to be overcome, not least as taxation issues must be settled by a unanimous vote in the Council of Ministers. Whatever the complexity of the detail, the Commission should receive the support of consumer representatives in trying to achieve its objectives, which will benefit a minority of consumers without damaging the interests of the majority.

Protecting Personal Financial Information

There is an increasingly wide-ranging debate about the privacy of the individual in modern society and what it means in terms of public policy. Is privacy a right? If so, how can the individual exercise this right in practice? If the right to privacy is qualified rather than absolute, in what circumstances do the needs of the state or the rights of others override the right of the individual?

One strand of the debate concerns the '... freedom from intrusion upon oneself, one's home, family and relationships' (Younger Committee 1972). For example, what limits, if any, should be put on the press, television and radio focusing the spotlight of publicity on the lives of private individuals? What constraints should there be on doorstep selling, when the commercial nature of the transaction may be masked by the relationship of host and guest? Should the use of the telephone for direct selling be allowed – and if so, subject to what constraints?

While these questions are relevant to financial services – especially to their marketing and selling – the second strand of the debate is of even greater importance. What right does one have '... to determine for oneself how and to what extent information about oneself is communicated to others'? (Younger Committee 1972). Of course, some personal information or data is normally publicly available – for example, name, address and telephone number. Most personal financial data – for example, bank account transactions – is not, for the good reason that people are sensitive about who holds information about their financial position and activities and how that information is used.

The issues underlying control of the flow of personal data are not new. They have been brought into prominence in public policy terms principally by the development of new computer and communications technologies. These make it easier for institutions to collect, store, process, retrieve and communicate personal data about identified individual consumers. The new technologies make it possible for institutions to deal with vast amounts of data very rapidly. They also make it possible to put together data from a number of different sources, published and unpublished, to build up a 'profile' of an individual consumer. This profile may be used for marketing goods or services which are unrelated to the sources of the original data. The profile of an individual consumer – income, account balances, pattern of expenditure, payment cards held, travel, subscriptions – may itself become a marketable commodity, which can be bought and sold without the knowledge of the individual concerned.

The development of new electronic payment methods has added to the kinds of personal data which can be stored and processed. If the consumer pays by cash, the transaction is anonymous. There is no record of the transaction which can be traced by the retailer or by a financial institution to the consumer. If the consumer pays by cheque, again the transaction is relatively anonymous. However, if the consumer pays by EFTPOS (Electronic Funds Transfer at Point of Sale), then information about the place and time of the transaction, the name of the retailer, the goods or services bought, and the amount paid can all be stored and processed electronically. Even a withdrawal from an ATM (Automated Teller Machine) discloses where the consumer was at a particular time.

Consumer Disquiet

There is evidence of consumer disquiet, especially about the use of personal financial data for commercial purposes, from a study carried out by the UK National Consumer Council, based on research into the attitudes of a national random sample of 1,071 consumers (*Taking Liberties*? 1988). In response to a question about whether a bank or building society should be allowed to pass personal financial data to a completely separate company, 52 per cent said that this should *never* be allowed, while a further 44 per cent stated that it should only be allowed with the consumer's full knowledge and consent.

The survey showed that consumers also have doubts about the use of personal financial data *within* a bank or building society. 14 per cent said that personal financial data should never be transferred to a bank or building society's own mortgage or investment division, and another 65 per cent believed that this should only be done with the consumer's full knowledge and consent. The comparable figures for passing information to a travel agent or estate agent owned by the bank or building society were 32 per cent and 60 per cent.

Within the same study, further research carried out in structured group discussions showed that UK consumers rate medical and financial information as the most sensitive and private categories of personal information and feel that the 'surrender' of such data makes them vulnerable. They very much disagree with the wide use made by financial institutions of the principle of 'implied consent', whereby the consumer is presumed to have given consent to the disclosure of financial data. Consumers are particularly opposed to the commercial use of their personal data – for example, the building up and use of mailing lists, and some direct selling. They feel that they are being exploited by the use of this information for anything other than the purpose for which it was collected and stored in the first place.

The issues involved in the internal use of personal data by banks and other financial institutions and its communication to third parties are examined in more detail below.

Internal Use by Banks and other Financial Institutions

Should there be any constraints on the extent to which a bank or other financial institution can use personal data for its own marketing purposes? The interaction of deregulation, increased competition and changing financial services markets means that in many Community countries the conventional boundaries between different types of financial institution are breaking down. The traditional 'core' services that banks provide to individual consumers are accepting deposits, making payments and extending credit, but more and more they are moving into the provision of other services – insurance, investment advice, portfolio management, estate agency (that is, selling houses and flats), even travel agency. Savings banks, whose operations have frequently been limited by statute, are now finding that they have the freedom to provide a wide range of banking services – as have building societies and similar mortgage credit institutions in some countries. Some insurance companies are eyeing the banking sector as a possible route for expansion. Of course, in a number of countries there are still statutory or regulatory obstacles to diversification, while many financial institutions, though given new freedoms, prefer to stick to the functions they know best. But the era of *bancassurance* or *allfinanz* is upon us and this has important consequences for the protection of personal data.

These consequences stem from the growing tendency of many banks and other financial institutions to turn themselves into conglomerates which provide a wide range of different financial services – and sometimes non-financial services as well. To what extent should a financial institution be allowed to use personal data which it necessarily has to collect to provide one service in marketing or selling a different, unrelated service?

An example from the UK puts the question into sharp focus. The personal customers of Midland Bank now have a standard set of terms and conditions which provides a contractual framework within which the bank provides its services. One of those terms and conditions is: 'We may disclose information about you to other companies in Midland Group'. A large travel agency, Thomas Cook, is part of the Midland Group. The effect of this contractual term, therefore, is that Midland Bank reserve the right to transfer personal data about the consumer's banking operations to the travel agency company. The personal financial data which Midland Bank have collected about the consumer in the course of providing her or him with banking services is now in principle available to a travel agency as a basis for marketing or selling travel services to that same consumer.

In the light of consumers' unease about the uses which are made of personal data, this must be unacceptable. On the other hand, it would surely be going too far to maintain that a bank should not be able to draw on its information about how a customer has operated an account in deciding whether or not to extend credit. Perhaps the practical solution is to draw a ring fence around the 'core' banking services of accepting deposits, making payments and extending credit. Banks would not be permitted to use personal data necessarily collected in performing those services in marketing or selling 'non-core' services without the consumer's explicit and informed consent. This is the principle that is followed in the Council of Europe Recommendation on protection of payment-related data, examined in detail below, and at least it would provide some safeguards.

External Disclosure of Personal Financial Data
The principle of the banker's duty of confidentiality is found in all EC member countries. In some, it is laid down in statute law, while in others it derives from case law established by the courts. For example, in the

UK the legal rather than the moral duty of the banker to maintain confidentiality was laid down in a celebrated legal case, known as the Tournier case (1924), which forms the cornerstone of common law in this field. Briefly, the court held that the duty of confidentiality came into existence along with the relationship between bank and customer and covers all information which the bank has acquired about the customer in the course of carrying out its banking duties. Four exceptions were identified to this implied contractual duty of confidentiality:

- Where disclosure is under compulsion by law;
- Where there is a duty to the public to disclose;
- Where the interests of the bank require disclosure;
- Where the disclosure is made by the express or implied consent of the customer.

Broadly similar qualifications to the banker's duty of confidentiality are found in many other national legal jurisdictions (Poullet 1990).

The Review Committee on Banking Services Law and Practice (1989) has raised the question as to whether these exceptions to the banker's duty of confidentiality are closely enough defined for today's changed circumstances, or whether their generality does not leave them open to abuse. For example, in relation to disclosure under compulsion by law and the duty to the public to disclose, the Review Committee comments that:

> 'The last two decades have seen a torrent of new legislation, which has become a spate in the last few years, requiring or permitting bankers, in a wide range of specified situations, to disclose confidential information in the public interest. Disclosure may be to the Government, or in some cases to the courts.'

The Review Committee goes on to identify 20 separate statutes requiring or permitting banks to disclose confidential customer information, in varied situations such as insider dealing, company fraud, insolvency, drug trafficking, breaches of the Consumer Credit Act 1974, tax evasion, inquiries into the affairs of charities, extradition, mental incapacity and the prevention of terrorism. It concludes that '... they constitute a serious inroad into the whole principle of customer confidentiality as conceived at the time of Tournier.'

So far as the other two Tournier exceptions are concerned, involving the interests of the bank and consent of the consumer, the UK Review Committee says that in practice banks usually rely on the implied consent of their customers for disclosures in the interests of the bank. It identifies the growth of private credit reference agencies in the UK and the possible disclosure to them by banks of personal financial data as a key issue.

The UK Review Committee concludes by recommending that the duty of confidentiality should be laid down in legislation, making it clear that the duty applies to *any* provider of banking services. All existing statutory exceptions from the duty of confidentiality, which are at present distributed in a wide variety of statutes, should be consolidated in the new law, which should not otherwise provide for any exception on the grounds of duty to the public. The circumstances in which the third exception – where the interests of the bank require disclosure – could be invoked should be tightly specified. The fourth exception should be altered to read 'where the disclosure is made by the express consent of the customer', the significance of this being that banks would no longer be able to rely on the consumer's implied consent. The Review Committee says that to qualify as express consent, the consumer must give consent in writing and must state the purpose for which it has been given.

If implemented, the UK Review Committee's recommendations would be a major step forward in consumer protection in an area where consumers' anxieties seem to be justified by the erosion in confidentiality that has taken place in recent years. This is especially true of the insistence on the consumer's express consent for disclosing personal financial data. However, after heavy lobbying by banking organisations, the UK Government has decided to do nothing about this issue. It does not accept the Review Committee's analysis that there has been a massive erosion of the banker's duty of confidentiality through statutory exceptions. It says that it had been:

> '... impressed by the evidence given during the consultation by those who have argued that the so called 'Tournier rules' are clear, have worked well, and are widely understood by bankers, and that any attempts to codify them in legislation would at best be unnecessary, and at worst likely to introduce new difficulties and confusion.'
> (*Banking Services Law and Practice – Government Response* 1990)

In rejecting a statutory approach, the UK Government has missed an opportunity to reassure consumers and enhance consumer protection in a way which would have presented few serious difficulties to banks and other financial institutions providing banking services. Its only concession is to say that a banking code of practice should explain to consumers how the Tournier rules on confidentiality work.

Council of Europe Data Protection Convention

At international level, the lead has been taken by the Council of Europe, an inter-governmental body with 21 member countries, including all EC countries. The Council of Europe Convention for the Protection of Individuals with regard to Automatic Processing of Personal Data (1981) is a major milestone in establishing the data protection rights of the individual. It is still the only international, legally binding instrument in the field of data protection.

The explicit object of the Convention is to strengthen data protection in relation to *automatic* data processing. It does not cover manually processed files. The Convention sets out basic principles along the following lines:

- Automatically processed personal data should be:
  – collected and processed fairly and lawfully;
  – stored for specified and lawful purposes and not used in a way incompatible with those purposes;
  – adequate, relevant and not excessive in relation to the purposes for which they are stored;
  – accurate and, where necessary, kept up to date;
  – held no longer than is necessary for the specified purpose.
- Personal data revealing racial origin, political opinions or religious or other beliefs, as well as personal data concerning health or sexual life, should not be processed automatically unless national law provides appropriate safeguards. This also applies to personal data about criminal convictions.
- Appropriate security measures should be taken for the protection of personal data against accidental or unauthorised destruction or accidental loss as well as against unauthorised access, alteration or dissemination.
- Anybody should be able:
  – to establish the existence of a personal data file and its main purpose, as well as the name and address of the 'controller of the file' (that is, the person or organisation which takes decisions about the file, its existence and contents);
  – to confirm whether her or his personal data are stored in the data file and to obtain a copy;
  – to correct or erase any personal data that have been processed contrary to these basic principles;

– to have a remedy if a request for confirmation or communication, correction or erasure is not complied with.

The Convention makes it clear that its provisions are not intended to preclude consumers being given a greater degree of data protection. It also covers the transfer of personal data across national boundaries. The provisions include but are not limited to personal financial data.

A number of EC countries have data protection legislation consistent with the Council of Europe Convention, some of which actually antedates the Convention itself. For example, in France, the Data Processing, Data Files and Individual Liberties Act came into force in January 1978. There is an independent data protection authority – the Commission Nationale de l'Information et des Libertés (CNIL) which regulates, monitors and oversees data protection. In Germany, the Federal Data Protection Act came into force in 1977. In the UK, the Convention has been implemented by the Data Protection Act 1984, which incorporates a set of principles whose wording differs from the principles set out in the Council of Europe Convention but whose substance is much the same. Enforcement responsibilities lie with the Data Protection Registrar whose responsibilities and powers are set out in the Act.

However, the Convention, a formal instrument of international law, has still not been ratified by Belgium, Italy, Greece and Portugal. None of these countries has national legislation which meets the standards laid down in the Convention. Spain has ratified the Convention, but not implemented it in national legislation. The Netherlands has introduced satisfactory national legislation but has not yet formally ratified the Convention. It is deplorable that so many member countries of the EC have taken no effective action in relation to the 1981 Council of Europe Convention, despite a 10-year-old recommendation from the Commission that they should do so.

Also, while the principles of the 1981 Council of Europe Convention are an excellent starting point, they do not in themselves provide a clear and precise legal framework within which institutions and consumers can be reasonably confident about their respective rights and obligations. Indeed, the Council of Europe itself has recognised the need for the principles of the 1981 Convention to be elaborated in the subsequent work it has carried out, by applying them to particular problem areas.

Council of Europe Recommendation on
Data Protection and Payments

An important example of this approach in the financial services field is the Recommendation for the Protection of Personal Data used for Payment or other Related Operations, which was approved by the Committee of Ministers of the Council of Europe on 13 September 1990. This Recommendation to the governments of member countries of the Council of Europe deals with a number of thorny problems in a very detailed way. It lays down guidelines for the way that data protection should be handled when consumers are paying for goods and services. These guidelines are valuable in themselves, but they might well also be a model for data protection principles and practices in other aspects of financial services.

The Recommendation covers any payment method whose use by individual consumers involves the automated processing of personal data. This obviously includes the use of electronic methods of payment involving the use of credit and debit cards in electronic terminals such as Automated Teller Machines (ATMs) and Electronic Funds Transfer at Point of Sale (EFTPOS), as well as home banking. It also includes paper-based payment methods, such as cheques and credit cards used in manual systems, if these at some stage involve automated processing. As hand written bank ledgers and index cards have virtually disappeared from the banking scene, it is safe to say that all payment methods other than cash are covered by the Recommendation – or will be within a year or two. The explanation of the Recommendation which follows is presented in terms of a card issuing financial institution providing a consumer with a payment card, but it should be remembered that the scope of the provisions ranges much wider than payment cards.

All 'bodies providing means of payment' come within the scope of the Recommendation. This means that, in the case of payment cards, for example, issuers such as building societies, retailers and petrol companies are included, as well as banks. This is an important element of consumer protection over and above the banker's duty of confidentiality referred to previously, which does not necessarily cover non-bank institutions. Another way in which the recommendation differs from the banker's duty of confidentiality is that it covers all aspects of the automated processing of personal data, not just the communication of personal data to others.

The Recommendation and accompanying explanatory memorandum make it clear that any card issuing institution should only *collect and store* personal data necessary for making the card available to the consumer and for providing the services linked to its use. Necessary data might include the consumer's name, address, age, sex, occupation and salary, and any other data needed to assess the risk involved in issuing the card. The individual consumer should be the primary source of the data, but there is no constraint on consulting publicly available sources such as electoral registers or telephone directories, to check whether or not individual consumers are who they say they are, the address given is correct, and so on. However, card issuers are warned against asking consumers to complete lengthy questionnaires requiring information which is quite unrelated to a decision on whether a card will be issued or not.

It is recognised that a card issuer may have to consult a third party, such as a credit reference agency, so as to assess the risk involved and store the data that such consultation involves. If this is likely to happen, the consumer should be told about the possibility that non-public sources may be consulted, the types of sources which may be consulted as well as the conditions under which such consultations may take place. The consumer should be free to withhold consent to this, but any consequential risks of this refusal – for example, that a decision may be taken not to issue a payment card – should be pointed out.

The Recommendation puts boundaries round the storage of personal data by retailers and service providers whom the consumer is paying when using a payment card. It recognises that the retailer may need to ask the consumer for proof of identity, contact the card issuer to check the consumer's solvency or credit limit, or check against lists of lost or stolen cards. It accepts that some data storage may be necessary to carry out these tasks, but states that personal data over and above the necessary minimum should not be stored by the retailer or service provider. Conversely, when personal data arise from the consumer's use of the card, the Recommendation provides that the card issuer should not store any such data over and above what is strictly necessary for validating and carrying out the transaction. There is no need for the card issuer to store data about the nature of the transaction.

When it comes to the *use* of personal data collected and stored by the card issuer, the Recommendation limits usage to the decision to provide a payment card, to managing the consumer's account and to dealing with the loss or theft of the card. There is, however, one important exception. The possible use by banks and other institutions of personal data for marketing and selling other services has already been raised above. The Recommendation deals with this by requiring the consumer to be told in writing in advance that personal data may be used as a basis for marketing and selling its range of services – for example, savings schemes, investment services and travel packages. The consumer should also be told that she or he has a right to refuse to appear on such a mailing list or lists and that if this right is exercised it will in no way affect the decision either to issue a payment card or to allow its continued use.

If the consumer agrees to being put on a mailing list, the card issuer may then use 'profiling' or other file interconnection techniques as a basis for marketing or selling its services to her or him. If such techniques are used for other purposes, though, it should only be with the express and informed consent of the individual (unless national law provides otherwise).

The Recommendation lays down firm principles for the *communication* of personal data for purposes other than those for which they are collected and stored. It states that data may only be communicated in the following cases:

- In accordance with obligations laid down by national law. These include response to a court order as well as any statutory duty to disclose personal financial data to the tax authorities or the police;
- When it is necessary to protect the essential and legitimate interests of the card issuer, for example in recovering money owed by the consumer or putting a card number on a 'stoplist' circulated to retailers. It is pointed out that the relevant interests of the card issuer should clearly outweigh the privacy interests of the consumer for this exception to be invoked;
- With the express and informed consent of the consumer. The implied consent of the consumer does not satisfy this requirement;
- If the consumer defaults in payment or exceeds a stipulated credit limit, the notification of this to any system for reporting or recording this type of information which has been set up in accordance with national law.

The Recommendation's restrictions on the communication of personal data do not only relate to transmitting data to third parties. They apply to other companies or divisions within the card issuer's group which are providing services unrelated to the provision of means of payment. The examples of travel firms and insurance companies are mentioned specifically in the Explanatory Memorandum which accompanies the Recommendation. Putting this in the context of the UK Midland Bank Group terms and conditions mentioned above, this means that if personal data about the consumer's use of a Midland Bank payment card were to be communicated to the travel agency within the Midland Bank Group, Thomas Cook, it would be contrary to the Recommendation unless the consumer's express and informed consent had been obtained.

The Recommendation also includes provisions comparable with those in the 1981 Convention on the consumer's right of access to personal data about herself or himself and the conditions under which the consumer has a right to have personal data corrected or erased. It also deals with the security and conservation of personal data connected with payments.

At international level, the Recommendation states that there should in principle be no obstacles to the cross-border flow of payment-related personal data between countries which have ratified the 1981 Convention, as there will be equivalent – though not necessarily identical – levels of data protection. The free flow of personal data to a country which has not ratified the 1981 Convention should depend on whether it respects the principles set out in the Recommendation.

Unlike the 1981 Convention, the Recommendation is not a legally binding instrument of international law. However, it does have considerable significance for the protection of personal data in the field of financial services, as it is the first attempt – and a successful one – to apply the framework of the Convention to a particular problem area. While it is confined to payment-related personal data, it is a good model for other aspects of financial services.

From the consumer viewpoint, there are three ways in which the Recommendation represents a significant advance in consumer protection:

• It rejects the notion of institutions being able to rely on the consumer's implied consent for certain uses and communication of personal data by insisting that the consumer's express and informed consent should be obtained;

• Personal data should only be used for marketing and selling if the consumer's express and informed consent has been obtained, and it is only after this that the institution concerned can engage in

profiling techniques as a basis for marketing or selling its other services to the consumer concerned;
* Restrictions on the communication of personal data apply not only to transmission to third parties but also to use in connection with non-payment activities of conglomerate institutions.

The European Commission's Approach

Until recently, the European Commission had seemed to be content to leave it to the Council of Europe to make the running on data protection issues. However, the failure of a number of EC member countries to implement the 1981 Council of Europe Convention and the wide diversity of approaches adopted by those which have implemented it have led the Commission to put forward a draft Directive on data protection (European Commision 1990i). Like the 1981 Council of Europe Convention, the draft Directive is intended to apply across the whole range of personal data, and is not limited either to financial services or payment-related data.

The objective of the draft EC Directive is to establish an equivalent, high level of data protection in all Community countries, so as to remove the obstacles to the cross- border flows of personal data that are a necessary component of an effective single market. While its principles are closely aligned with those established by the Council of Europe, there are other differences which are important:

* The draft EC Directive covers both manual and automated data files, while the Council of Europe Convention (and Rec-ommendation on payment-related data) exclude manually processed data. If this aspect of the draft Directive is retained, the scope of some existing national data protection laws, such as the UK Data Protection Act 1984, would have to be extended to cover manual as well as automated data;
* The draft EC Directive deals separately and in some respects differently with the public and private sectors.

The draft EC Directive is being strongly criticised by many commercial interests. For example, one of the Commission's own advisory bodies claims that ' ... it would bring into force regulation more restrictive than any regime in operation in any member state or indeed in any country in the world' (Committee on Commerce and Distribution 1991a). The draft is under attack because it would involve rewriting much existing national legislation which is said to be working well – and, not least, because it would seem to prohibit some existing practices, such as profiling and credit scoring of consumers' applications for credit. Its cause is not helped by ambiguities and roughness in the first draft.

The text is not examined in detail here, because a revised draft will undoubtedly appear before long. However, it has precipitated a debate over the best method of achieving effective protection of data. Civil libertarians tend to look on maximum protection codified in legislation to be in the best interests of the consumer. This view is reflected in the first draft of the EC Directive. Some consumer representatives take the view that the consumer should exercise control over her or his data and decide how it can be used. This position relies on the concept of 'informed consent'. Central to the effective functioning of informed consent is consumer access to all the information necessary to make the decision. Consumers must then be given the opportunity to make a decision.

In practice, this means consumers must be told why information is being collected and how it might be used. If there are uses beyond the primary purposes for collecting the information, the consumer must be able to stop these secondary applications. There are two ways of doing this. One is called positive option or 'opt-in', the other is negative option or 'opt-out'. Under the opt-in method, no personal data can be used for marketing purposes unless the consumer has given her or his personal consent in advance. Under the opt-out method, personal data can be used for marketing purposes until the consumer asks that it is not used in this way.

Most civil libertarians and many consumer representatives favour the opt-in approach. However, in its submission on the first draft of the EC Directive, the UK National Consumer Council, while supporting the general thrust of the proposals, does not agree with the Commission's adoption of the opt-in approach (National Consumer Council 1991). Certainly, firms which rely on personal information to develop marketing lists claim that the opt-in approach would raise the cost of direct marketing and could even lead to increases in junk mail. As direct marketing is claimed to be one of the primary ways in which consumers throughout the EC will obtain access to a single market for goods and services, any unnecessary constraints on direct marketing may help confine consumers to local markets.

The opt-in method, of course, relies on firms conforming to high standards of best practice – and many firms claim that they do already use high standards. There is thus considerable pressure on the Commission to change its approach in revising its draft proposals. It is not an easy issue on which to reach an optimum framework which takes account of the best interests of both firms and consumers. The Commission will need to be vigilant in ensuring that any change in approach does not erode consumer interests. A complicating factor is that some consumer organisations (not, it should be said, the UK National Consumer Council) are themselves heavy users of direct mail in promoting membership and subscriptions and therefore have a foot in both camps.

One point worth noting is that the present text provides for the exercise of sectoral rule-making powers by the Commission. The special sensitivity of personal financial data means that specific rules for the financial services sector should be high on the Commission's agenda once the Directive has been adopted.

The Consumer Agenda
Developments in computer technology have led to a growing realisation of the high commercial value of personal data as a basis for marketing and selling financial services. The traditional approach of the banker's duty of confidentiality, while it should not be discarded, appears more and more limited as a way of safeguarding the privacy of consumers – especially as the range of institutions providing financial services goes well beyond the definition of a bank. Consumers' rights need both a clearly defined statutory framework and a continuing administrative system – such as the CNIL in France and the Data Protection Registrar in the UK – for making sure that these rights can be exercised effectively.

The 1981 Council of Europe Convention is proving to be the foundation on which national and international data protection systems are built. The 1990 Council of Europe Recommendation on payment-related personal data is an important step forward in the financial services sector. It deserves close attention both in its own right and as a model for other aspects of data protection in financial services.

However, the situation at European Community level is extremely unsatisfactory. A number of EC countries have so far failed to implement the Council of Europe Convention and have either inadequate or no relevant legislation. The Commission is therefore fully justified in putting forward proposals for a Directive which would set high standards for national legislation and which would incorporate a high level of consumer protection. Despite the imperfections of the first draft of the Directive, the principles it embodies should be strongly supported by those representing consumers' interests.

The Way Ahead

The potential benefits that completion of the single market for financial services could bring to European consumers are considerable. They could come in the form of wider choice of financial services, wider choice of financial institutions and lower prices. The scope of the benefits would of course vary widely from country to country and from financial service to financial service.

In practice, the benefits may well turn out to be appreciably less than the ideal of a single market would suggest. While the Commission's overall strategy of essential harmonisation, mutual recognition and home country control seems to be broadly in the interests of the Community's consumers, the detailed provisions of many of the proposals are being diluted because of opposition from individual member countries or lobbying by the financial services industries themselves. Also, the protection of consumer interests is sometimes at risk because it is not always conceived as being part of the 'essential harmonisation'. It has sometimes seemed as though the single market for financial services was being built solely in the interests of financial institutions (see for example Bank of England 1989).

Another constraint stems from the behaviour of the financial institutions themselves. Many of them seem to want to avoid the costs and hazards of direct international competition and are preparing for the 'single' European market with acquisitions, mergers, alliances and networks which will help to cushion its impact. The worst outcome for consumers would be a series of European super-bank alliances actively protecting high margins in separate national markets. However, one of the consequences of building a single European market will be to stimulate keener competition in the over-regulated financial services markets in many member countries.

Inadequate Consultation

In this complex and very rapidly changing situation, it has been difficult for representatives of the interests of consumers to get into the action at an early enough stage and with sufficient clout to influence developments in favour of consumers. Some of the problems are familiar. As always, consumer organisations are handicapped by not having enough people and enough money for effective lobbying. Some are distinct to this situation. For example, the pressure of time on the Commission to complete the framework by end-1992 means that some Commission officials are anxious to do deals at an early stage with their respective financial services sectors to avoid trouble and opposition that will cause delays. There has been an unhappy record, only recently put right, of Commission officials neglecting to consult consumer interests and not making working documents available to consumer organisations.

The consumer interest is therefore often left to airy generalisations and optimistic forecasts about the effects of competition, while the often crucial small print takes little account of the need for safeguarding both enhanced consumer choice and effective consumer protection. Another factor which has weighed against consumers is that the Commission's Consumer Policy Service, which is responsible for promoting and protecting consumers' interests, is itself short of resources. While its staff have been vigorous in promoting its own initiatives on consumer credit and payment cards, it is only recently that it has been seriously concerned with trying to ensure that proposals on financial services coming from other parts of the Commission – notably, DG XV, the Directorate General responsible for financial institutions – are sensitive to consumer needs.

The inadequacies of consultation at European level have been mirrored at national level in the failure of many governments of member countries to take account of the consumer interest when developing their attitude towards proposals coming from the Commission. In the UK, this attracted the attention of a Parliamentary Committee, which was moved to recommend that the government '... should, as a matter of course, consult formally with consumer groups on all developments concerning the single market' (House of Commons 1989).

However, consultative procedures are now improved, at both the European level and in some member countries. While the main lines of the Commission's strategy are now both clear and unchangeable, there is still much to be achieved if the single European market for financial services is to benefit consumers as well as financial institutions. The section at the end of each preceding chapter on The Consumer Agenda focuses on the specific issues which still need to be resolved to make the single market work for consumers. The three issues singled out below – the consumer's freedom to buy, competition policy and effective consumer redress and compensation – are common to the whole range of financial services.

The Fourth Freedom – the Consumer's Freedom to Buy

The chapter on The Grand Design identified the Commission's strategy as being based on three freedoms which will transcend the Community's internal frontiers. These are the freedom of movement of capital, the freedom of establishment of financial institutions and the freedom of financial institutions to supply services. The consumer's freedom to *buy* financial services across frontiers is not stated explicitly. It may be that it is in principle implicit in some of the Commission's initiatives, especially the Liberalisation of Capital Movements Directive.

However, it is a freedom which is at present seriously limited in a number of member countries. Consumers may be prohibited from opening a bank account, getting a house mortgage or taking out life insurance in another Community country, or face unfavourable tax treatment if they do so. Also, there is nothing in the Commission's initiatives to prevent a financial institution from refusing to supply a financial service to a consumer on grounds of nationality or residence. The emphasis throughout all the measures that have been adopted or are under discussion is on the freedom of the financial institution: there is little or none on the freedom of the consumer. It is time that the Commission took steps to build a fourth freedom into its strategy – the freedom of the consumer to buy financial services without national or residential discrimination.

Vigorous Competition

Many financial institutions are planning to minimise the competitive impact of the completion of the single market. The role of the competition policy agencies at European and national levels will become increasingly important in ensuring that consumers get the benefits of competition. Fortunately, many of the exemptions that the banking and insurance industries have had from national competition legislation are being questioned. The financial services sector is attracting the attention of the Commission's competition policy arm, Directorate General IV, and national competion agencies, where they exist. Consumers of financial services can only benefit from vigorous pro-competitive action and consumer organisations should see this as a priority issue.

Effective Consumer Redress and Compensation

Consumers need quick, low-cost and effective disputes resolution procedures for financial services. They also need to know that they will be properly compensated if financial institutions become insolvent. The situation is unsatisfactory throughout the Community. Even in the UK, where there are complaint and redress schemes covering insurers, banks and building societies, they all have different terms of reference and procedures. The new schemes introduced by the self-regulatory organisations under the Financial Services Act 1986 all differ from each other in quite significant respects.

Elsewhere in the Community, the situation is even less satisfactory, though there are industry-based complaints schemes for both insurance and banking in Denmark and the Netherlands and for banking in Belgium and Ireland. There is major uncertainty about how cross-border disputes about financial services will be resolved, either within or outwith the judicial system (Thomas and Weatherill 1991).

Some member countries have no effective arrangements for compensating consumers if a financial institution fails. Where there are arrangements, they differ markedly from country to country. The development of minimum harmonised levels of compensation – and standardised procedures for meeting claims – throughout the Community is surely a necessary condition for the single market for financial services.

None of the measures that has been adopted appears to make any provision for the resolution of cross-border disputes about financial services. The provisions for dealing with compensation claims are hopelessly inadequate. Consumer redress and compensation should be priority issues for the Commission. The inadequacy of the present situation has been highlighted by the July 1991 forced closure of the Bank of Credit and Commerce International.

A Final Assessment

'1992' is not a magic talisman. There will be no overnight transformation on New Year's Day, 1993. For consumers, the single European market for financial services will be slow in arriving. For many years to come, there will constraints and impediments which will limit the scope for wider choice and lower prices. Differences in national legislation and the culture of money will persist. Eventually, though – perhaps not until the next millenium – things will change. The framework for a single market is in place, even though many of the details remain to be filled in. Many of those details are highly significant for consumers. There is still an opportunity for consumers and their representatives to make sure that they, too, share some of the benefits of the single market for financial services.

However, it would not be wise for consumers and their representatives to be too optimistic about the extent to which the European Community is prepared to take account of their needs and interests. In its decision on 25 July 1991 about the draft budget of the Commission for 1992, the Council of Ministers decided that the amount of money available to the Consumer Policy Service, which has the job of representing consumer interests within the Commission, should be slashed to 4.347 million ECU from the 1991 figure of 10.805 million ECU. Among other cuts, this will involve:

• Cutting off financial support to consumer organisations;
• Cancelling plans for developing consumer representation in Ireland and Southern Europe;
• Dissolving the CCC (Consumers' Consultative Council);
• Stopping all new studies of how the single market will affect consumers;
• Closing down trans-border consumer information centres and projects for resolving consumer complaints.

This severe blow to the promotion of consumer interests within the single European market must raise grave doubts about the reality behind the honeyed words of the EC's leaders that the single market is intended to benefit consumers. More than ever, consumers will have to work hard to ensure that their own interests are safeguarded and promoted – and in particular that the single market for financial services represents a consumer benefit rather than a banker's racket.

References and Bibliography

Abbey National (1990), *Survey on Information about Bank Charges*, April, London.

Actualité Bancaire (19 February 1990), Association Française des Banques, Paris.

Advertisements and Quotations Regulations (1989) – Consumer Credit (Advertisements) Regulations 1989 SI 1125 and Consumer Credit (Quotations) Regulations 1989 SI 1126, HMSO, London.

Allix, Jean (1989), 'The Consumer's View of the EPS Ad Hoc Group Report', in CEN (1989) – q.v.

Allix, Jean (1990a), 'Banking Proposals, Payment Methods and Consumer Protection', in Mitchell, Jeremy, ed. (1990) *The Consumer and Financial Services* – q.v.

Allix, Jean (1990b), 'Porteurs de Cartes – Une Nouvelle Protection', in *Bancatique*, 66, December, Paris.

Amex Bank Review (3 April 1991), 18, 3, 'Regulation of Financial Services', London.

Andrews, Ann (1988), 'The UK Borrower, Money Advice and the Need for Reform', in Mitchell, Jeremy, ed. (1988c) *Money and the Consumer* – q.v.

Association Française des Banques (1987), *La Concurrence Bancaire en France et en Europe*, Paris.

Bank of England (1989), *The Single European Market – Survey of the UK Financial Services Industry*, London.

Banking Ombudsman Scheme (1990), *Annual Report 1989-90*, London.

Banking Services Law and Practice – the Government's Response (1990), Cmd 1026, HMSO, London.

Battelle Institute (1989), 'Untenable Card Differences in Europe', in *Battelle on Automated Banking in Europe*, 84, March, London.

Battelle Institute (1990), 'Europe is Closing ATM Gap', in *Battelle on Automated Banking in Europe*, 100, November/December, London.

Battelle Institute (1991), 'Payments – a Decade of Change', in *Battelle on Automated Banking in Europe*, 104, May, London.

Berthoud, Richard (1990), 'Credit Use and Debt Problems in the UK', in Mitchell, Jeremy, ed. (1990) *The Consumer and Financial Services* – q.v.

Bourgoignie, Thierry and Goyens, Monique, eds. (1990), *Electronic Funds Transfer and Consumer Protection*, Story-Scientia, Brussels.

Brittan, Sir Leon (1990a), *European Insurance in a Single Market*, speech to Centre for Insurance Sciences, University of Leuwen, 19 March.

Brittan, Sir Leon (1990b), *Unifying Europe's Financial Markets*, speech to the European Commission Conference on Banking and Insurance, 15 October, Brussels.

Broadcasting Support Services (1989), *Money, Credit and Debt*, Project report No.1, British Broadcasting Corporation, London.

Bröker, Gunther (1989), *Competition in Banking*, OECD, Paris.

Building Societies Association (1990), *Building Societies and 1992*, 2nd edition, London.

Building Societies' Ombudsman Scheme (1990), *Annual Report 1989-90*, London.

Bureau Européen des Unions de Consommateurs (1988a), *Term Insurance in Europe*, Brussels.

Bureau Européen des Unions de Consommateurs (1988b), *Transfer of Money within the EEC*, BEUC/76/88, Brussels.

Bureau Européen des Unions de Consommateurs (1988c), *Holiday Money*, BEUC/1/88, Brussels.

CEN – European Committee for Standardisation (1989), *Workshop Proceedings – European Standardisation of Transaction Cards*, Brussels.

Comité Consultatif (1989), *Rapport 1988-89*, Conseil National du Crédit, Paris.

Committee on Commerce and Distribution of the European Commission (1991a), *Preliminary Opinion on the Proposal for a Council Directive on the Protection of Personal Data*, Brussels.

Committee on Commerce and Distribution of the European Commission (1991b), *Draft Code of Practice relating to Electronic Payment in particular the relationship between Card Issuers and Acceptors*, Brussels.

Committee on Commerce and Distribution of the European Commission (1991c), *Draft Code of Practice concerning Payment Systems, and in particular the relationship between Cardholders and Card Issuers*, Brussels.

Consumer Consultative Committee of the European Commission (1989), *Avis concernant la transparence des conditions de banque applicable aux transactions transfrontalières*, CCC/31/89, Brussels.

Consumer Consultative Committee of the European Commission (1990), *Opinion Rejecting the Code of Good Conduct of the Three European Banking Organisations in the Field of Electronic Payment*, CCC/040/90, Brussels.

Consumer Credit Act (1974), HMSO, London.

Consumers in the European Community Group (1990a), *Comments on the European Commission's Discussion Paper: Making Payments in the Internal Market*, London.

Consumers in the European Community Group (1990b), *Comments on the DTI Consultative Document: EC Capital Adequacy Directive*, London.

Contract Conditions Act AGB Gesetz/Gesetz zur Regelung der allegemein Geschaftsbedingungen, Bonn.

Council of Europe (1981), *Convention for the Protection of Individuals with regard to Automatic Processing of Personal Data*, Strasbourg.

Council of Europe (1990), *Recommendation for the Protection of Personal Data used for Payment or other Related Operations*, Strasbourg.

Council of Mortgage Lenders (1990), *Housing Finance Fact Book*, London.

Court of Justice (1986), Case 205/84, *ECR* 3755 at 3803 No.30 – European Commission v Germany.

Court of Justice (1987), Case 45/87, Verband der Sachversicherer v European Commission.

Daily Herald (1 February 1991), Glasgow.

Data Protection Registrar (1991), *Comments on Draft EC General Directive on Data Protection*, Wilmslow, UK.

Department of Trade and Industry (1990a), *EC Investment Services Directive – a Consultative Document*, London.

Department of Trade and Industry (1990b), *Proposals for New Legislation on Credit Marketing*, London.

Department of Trade and Industry (1990c), *EC Capital Adequacy Directive – a Consultative Document*, London.

Department of Trade and Industry (1991), *EC Third Life Insurance (Framework) Directive – a Consultative Document*, London.

Dermine, Jean (1991), *The Gains from European Banking Integration*, Research Report No.6, Centre for European Policy Studies, Brussels.

Draft Code of Banking Practice (1990), British Bankers' Association, London.

ECPS – European Council for Payment Systems (1987), *European Accord for Bank Card Usage*.

ECSA – European Credit Sector Associations (1988), *Joint Comments on the Draft Proposal for a Council Directive Concerning Payment Systems and Protection of Consumers*, Brussels.

Electronic Payments International (April 1989), 31, 'Prepaid Cards' Popularity Prompts Regulatory Investigation', Dublin.

Elvinger, Andre (1988), 'The Investment Funds Regulations in Luxembourg', in *Les Fonds d'Investissement – Réglementation – Fiscalité – Evolution*, Association Luxembourgeoise des Juristes de Banque, Luxembourg.

Euromoney (April 1991), London.

European Banker (29 October 1990), 'Keep Your Tanks Off Our Lawn!', Dublin.

European Banking Federation (1990), *Observations on the Commission's Discussion Paper: Making Payments in the Internal Market*, Brussels.

European Commission (1984), *Decision on Uniform Eurocheques* of 10 December 1984, *OJ* L 35, 7 February 1985, Brussels.

European Commission (1985), *Completing the Internal Market White Paper from the Commission to the Council*, COM(85)310 of 14 June 1985, Brussels.

European Commission (1986), *Recommendation Concerning the Introduction of Deposit-Guarantee Schemes in the Community* (87/63/EEC) of 22 December 1986, *OJ* L 33, 4 February 1987, Brussels.

European Commission (1987a), *Europe Could Play an Ace: the New Payment Cards*, COM(86)754 final, Brussels.

European Commission (1987b), *Recommendation on a European Code of Conduct Relating to Electronic Payment* (87/598/EEC) of 8 December 1987, *OJ* L 365, 24 December 1987, Brussels.

European Commission (1987c), *Towards a Dynamic Economy – Green Paper on the Development of the Common Market for*

Telecommunications Services and Equipmen, COM(87)290 of 30 June 1987, Brussels.

European Commission (1988a), *Proposal for a Council Directive on the Reorganisation and Winding-Up of Credit Institutions and [on] Deposit Guarantee Schemes, OJ* C 36 of 8 February 1988, Brussels.

European Commission (1988b), *Recommendation Concerning Payment Systems* (88/590/EEC) of 24 November 1988, Brussels.

European Commission (1988c), *Telecommunications – Progress on the Definition of Open Network Provision,* COM(88)718 of 15 December 1988, Brussels.

European Commission (1988d), *Towards a European Market for the Undertakings for Collective Investment in Transferable Securities,* Brussels.

European Commission (1989a), *Proposal for a Council Directive on Investment Services in the Securities Field* of 3 January 1989, COM (88)778, *OJ* C 43, 22 February 1989, Brussels.

European Commission (1989b), *Proposal for a Council Directive on the Compulsory Winding-Up of Insurance Undertakings,* COM(89)394 final, *OJ* C 253, 6 October 1989, Brussels.

European Commission (1989c), *Proposal for a Council Regulation on the Application of Article 85(3) of the Treaty to Certain Categories of Agreements, Decisions and Concerted Practices in the Insurance Sector,* COM(89)641 final, *OJ* C 16, 23 January 1990, Brussels.

European Commission (1989d), *Proposal for a Council Directive on the Annual Accounts of Insurance Undertakings,* COM(89)474 final of 25 October 1989, *OJ* C 30, 8 February 1990, Brussels.

European Commission (1990b), *Amended Proposal for a Council Directive on Investment Securities in the Investment Services Field* of 23 January 1990, COM(89)629 final, *OJ* C 42, 22 February 1990, Brussels.

European Commission (1990c), *Recommendation on the Transparency of Banking Conditions Relating to Cross-Border Financial Transactions* (90/109/EEC) of 14 February 1990, *OJ* L 67, 15 March 1990, Brussels.

European Commission (1990d), *Proposal for a Third Council Directive on the Co-ordination of Laws, Regulations and Administrative Provisions Relating to Direct Insurance other than Life Assurance* (Proposal for a Third Non-Life Directive), COM(90)348 final, 27 July 1990, *OJ* C 244, 28 September 1990, Brussels.

European Commission (1990e), *Making Payments in the Internal Market*, COM(90)447 final, Brussels.

European Commission (1990f), *One Money, One Market*, European Economy 44, Brussels.

European Commission (1990g), *Proposal for a Council Directive on Capital Adequacy of Investment Firms and Credit Institutions*, COM (90)141 final, *OJ* C 152, 21 June 1990, Brussels.

European Commission (1990h), *Proposal for a Council Directive on Unfair Terms in Consumer Contracts*, COM(90)322 final, *OJ* C 243, 28 September 1990, Brussels.

European Commission (1990i), *Draft Proposal for a Council Directive Approximating Certain Laws, Regulations and Administrative Provisions of the Member States Concerning the Protection of Individuals in Relation to the Processing of Personal Data* SYN 287, Brussels.

European Commission (1990j), *Working Paper – Completing the Internal Market for Private Retirement Provisions* (mimeo), XV(90)224-EN, 23 October 1990, Brussels.

European Commission (1991), *Proposal for a Third Council Directive for the Co-ordination of Laws, Regulations and Administrative Provisions Relating to Direct Life Assurance* (Proposal for a Third Life Directive), COM(91)57 final, 25 February 1991, *OJ* C 99, 16 April 1991, Brussels.

European Community Directives (chronological order and abbreviated titles) -

> *First Motor Insurance Liability Directive* (72/116/EEC) of 24 April 1972, *OJ* L 103, 2 May 1972, Brussels.
>
> *First Non-Life Insurance Directive* (73/239/EEC) of 24 July 1973, *OJ* L 228, 16 August 1973, Brussels.
>
> *Insurance Intermediaries Directive* (77/92/EEC) of 13 December 1976, *OJ* L 26, 31 January 1977, Brussels.
>
> *First Banking Directive* (77/780/EEC) of 12 December 1977, *OJ* L 322, 17 December 1977, Brussels.
>
> *Co-Insurance Directive* (78/473/EEC) of 30 May 1978, *OJ* L 151, 7 June 1978, Brussels.
>
> *First Life Insurance Directive* (79/267/EEC) of 5 March 1979, *OJ* L 63, 13 March 1979, Brussels.
>
> *Second Motor Insurance Liability Directive* (84/5/EEC) of 30 December 1983, *OJ* L 8, 11 January 1984, Brussels.

Assistance Directive (84/641/EEC) of 10 December 1984, *OJ* L 339, 27 December 1984, Brussels.

UCITS Directive (85/611/EEC) of 20 December 1985, *OJ* L 375, 31 December 1985, Brussels.

Partial Capital Liberalisation Directive (86/566/EEC) of 17 November 1986, *OJ* L 332, 26 November 1986, Brussels.

Bank Accounts Directive (86/635/EEC) of 8 December 1986, *OJ* L 372, 31 December 1986, Brussels.

First Consumer Credit Directive (87/102/EEC) of 22 December 1986, *OJ* L 42, 12 February 1987, Brussels.

Legal Expenses Directive (87/344/EEC) of 22 June 1987, *OJ* L 185, 4 July 1987, Brussels.

Credit and Suretyship Insurance Directive (87/343/EEC) of 22 June 1987, *OJ* L 185, 4 July 1987, Brussels.

Second Non-Life Insurance Directive (88/357/EEC) of 22 June 1988, *OJ* L 172, 4 July 1988, Brussels.

Capital Liberalisation Directive (88/361/EEC) of 24 June 1988, *OJ* L 178, 8 July 1988, Brussels.

Bank Branches Directive (89/117/EEC) of 13 February 1989, *OJ* L 44, 16 February 1989, Brussels.

Own Funds Directive (89/299/EEC) of 17 April 1989, *OJ* L 124, 5 May 1989, Brussels.

Second Banking Directive (89/646/EEC) of 15 December 1989, *OJ* L 386, 30 December 1989, Brussels.

Solvency Ratios Directive (89/647/EEC) of 18 December 1989, *OJ* L, 30 December 1989, Brussels.

Second Consumer Credit Directive (90/80/EEC) of 22 February 1990, *OJ* L 61, 10 March 1990, Brussels.

Third Motor Insurance Liability Directive (90/232/EEC) of 14 May 1990, *OJ* L 129, 19 May 1990, Brussels.

Motor Insurance Services Directive (90/618/EEC) of 8 November 1990, *OJ* L 330, 29 November 1990, Brussels.

Second Life Insurance Directive (90/619/EEC) of 8 November 1990, *OJ* L 330, 29 November 1990, Brussels.

European Consumer Law Group (1986), *Consumers in Debt*, Brussels.

European Consumer Law Group (1990), 'Consumers and the Internal Market for Services: Shortcomings of the New Approach of the Community', in *Journal of Consumer Policy*, 13, 1, March.

Financial Services Act (1986), HMSO, London.

Financial Statistics (February 1991), HMSO, London.

Finance Houses Association (1987), *Code of Practice*, London.

Finsinger, Jörg; Hammond, Elizabeth and Tapp, Julian (1985), *Insurance – Competition or Regulation?*, Institute for Fiscal Studies, London.

Fitchew, Geoffrey (1988), 'Commission's Proposals for Achieving a Single Banking Market', speech to BRI Conference on the Changing Face of European Banking, 30 June, London.

Ford, Janet (1988), *The Indebted Society*, Routledge, London.

General Household Survey (1985), HMSO, London.

Glasgow Herald (1 February 1991).

Hinton, Teresa and Berthoud, Richard (1988), *Money Advice Services*, Policy Studies Institute, London.

House of Commons Trade and Industry Committee (1989), *Financial Services and the Single European Market*, HC 256, HMSO, London.

Housing Finance (1990), No.5, February, Council of Mortgage Lenders, London.

Insurance Intermediaries Act (1952), The Hague, The Netherlands.

INTAMIC (1990), *Pre-Paid Instrument Used in a Closed System – an Opportunity for the Banks*, London.

Journal Officiel (5 July 1989), Ministère de l'Economie, des Finances et du Budget, Paris.

Jubilee Centre (1988), *Families in Debt*, Cambridge.

Kessler, Denis ed.(1988), 'Is There an Optimal Usury Law?', in *Money and the Consumer*, ed. Mitchell, Jeremy, Money Management Council, London.

Knobbout-Bethlem, Charlotte (1990), *A Survey of the Implementation of the EC Recommendation Concerning Payment Systems*, Molengraaff Institute for Private Law, for Consumentenbond/BEUC, Utrecht.

Krakowski, Michael (1988), *Regulierung in der Bundesrepublik Deutschland*, Verlag Weltarchiv, Hamburg.

Le Crédit à la Consommation (1988), CRC, Lille, and CRIOC, Brussels.

Les Notes Bleues (28 May 1990), Ministère de l'Economie, des Finances et du Budget, Paris.

Maystadt, Philippe (1988), *Bilan et Perspective en Matière d'Assurances*, Ministère de l'Economie, Brussels.

Mitchell, Jeremy (1988a), *Electronic Banking and the Consumer – the European Dimension*, Policy Studies Institute, London.

Mitchell, Jeremy (1988b), 'New Payment Systems – a UK Consumer View' – q.v. reference immediately below.

Mitchell, Jeremy ed.(1988c), *Money and the Consumer – an International Review*, Money Management Council, London.

Mitchell, Jeremy (1989a), 'Credit Cards, New Technology and Consumer Debt', in *Journal of Consumer Studies and Home Economics*, 13, 4, 293- 306.

Mitchell, Jeremy (1989b), 'The Consumer Interest', in CEN (1989) – q.v.

Mitchell, Jeremy ed. (1990), *The Consumer and Financial Services – New Horizons*, Centre de Droit de la Consommation, Louvain-la-Neuve, and Center for Consumer Affairs, Milwaukee.

Mitchell, Jeremy (1991), 'Changing Structures and Changing Markets – New Opportunities and New Hazards for Consumers', in *Prometheus*, 8, 1, Univeristy of Queensland, Australia.

Moon, Michael (1989), *Regulatory Change in West German Financial Markets* (mimeo), European Policy Research Unit, University of Manchester.

National Consumer Council (1985), *Losing at Cards*, London.

National Consumer Council (1987), *Security Risks?*, London.

National Consumer Council (1988), *Taking Liberties?*, London.

National Consumer Council (1991), *Response to Home Office Consultative Document on the European Commission's First Draft Directive on Data Protection*, London.

Office of Fair Trading (1986), *The Selling of Insurance Policies*, London.

Office of Fair Trading (1988), *Consumers' Use of Credit*, London.

Office of Fair Trading (1989), *Overindebtedness*, London.

OECD – Organisation for Economic Co-operation and Development (1983), *International Trade in Services – Insurance*, Paris.

OECD – Organisation for Economic Co-operation and Development (1987), *Consumers and Life Insurance*, Paris.

Payment Cards Act (1984), Copenhagen.

People and Payments (1987), Lafferty Publications, Dublin.

Pool, Bill (1990), *The Creation of the Internal Market in Insurance*, Office for Official Publications of the European Community, Luxembourg.

Poullet, Yves (1990), 'TEF et Protection des Données a Caractère Personnel', in Bourgoignie, Thierry and Goyens, Monique, eds. (1990) – q.v.

Price Waterhouse (1988), *The Cost of Non-Europe in Financial Services*, London.

Price Waterhouse (February 1989), *Communiqué*, London.

Proposals for International Convergence of Capital Measurement and Capital Standards (1988), Cooke Committee Report, Bank for International Settlements, Basle.

Rapport Cortesse (1985), Ministère de l' Economie, des Finances et du Budget, Paris.

Report of the Committee on Privacy – Younger Committee (1972), HMSO, London.

Report of the Review Committee on Banking Services Law and Practice – Jack Committee (1989), Cmd 622, HMSO, London.

Retail Banker International (3 April 1989), 181, 'UCITS – Can Bankers Sell a Pan-European Fund?', Dublin.

Retail Banker International (10 September 1990), 215, 'Spanish Banks Blasted for Misleading Information', Dublin.

Retail Banker International (17 December 1990), 222, 'Plastic May Soothe European Bankers' Headaches', Dublin.

Retail Banker International (11 March 1991), 228, 'Dutch Distribution Row Continues', Dublin.

Retail Banker International (27 March 1991), 229, 'Deutsche Bank Executive Raps Insurance Regulators', Dublin.

Retail Banker International (27 May 1991), 233, 'Allfinanz Shows its Good and Bad Sides', Dublin.

Schmitz, Bob (1988), *The Changing Face of European Insurance – a Consumer View*, BEUC, Brussels.

Schmitz, Bob (1989), *Consumers and a Common Market in Financial Services by 1992 – Introductory Report on Insurance* (mimeo), BEUC, Brussels, and AgV, Bonn.

Schneider, Uwe and Troberg, Peter (1990), 'Finanzdienstleistungen im EG-Binnenmarkt; Sitzland oder Gastlandrecht?', in *Wertpapier Mitteilungen*, 5, 3, February.

Sigma (4, 1990), Swiss Reinsurance Company, Zurich.

Stanton, Elizabeth (1991), 'Recession, a Boom, and ... Another Recession', in *International Parallels*, 1, 1, April, New York.

The Economist (29 April 1989), 'European Unit Trusts – Invading British Beaches', London.

The Economist (24 February 1990), 'European Insurance – Getting Down to Business', London.

Thomas, Richard and Weatherill, Stephen (1991), 'Consumer Regulation across Borders', in *Consumer Policy Review*, 1, 1, January, London.

Tournier v National Provincial and Union Bank of England (1924), 1 KB 461.

Troberg, Peter (1990), 'Integration of EEC Payment Systems: European Commission Initiatives', speech to Banca d'Italia Conference, 23 November, Perugia.

Unemployment and Consumer Debts in Europe (1989), Institut für Finanzdienstleistungen, Hamburg.

Which? (October 1986), 'Life Insurance', Consumers' Association, London.

Which? (April 1990), 'A Fair Rate?', Consumers' Association, London.

Wiesner, Helena (1990), 'Redress for Consumer Grievances', in Mitchell, Jeremy, ed. (1990) *The Consumer and Financial Services* – q.v.

Glossary of Initials and Acronyms

ACH	Automated Clearing House: an institution which processes electronic debits and credits
AFB (Fr)	Association Française des Banques
AgV (Ger)	Arbeitsgemeinschaft der Verbraucherverbande: German consumer organisation
APACS	Association for Payment Clearing Services: UK umbrella organisation for payment clearing services
APR	Annual Percentage Rate of charge for credit
ATM	Automated Teller Machine: a terminal provided by a bank or other financial institution which enables the consumer to withdraw cash and which may have other uses, such as depositing cash and cheques or ordering a cheque book
BCCI	Bank of Credit and Commerce International
BAV (Ger)	Bundesaufsichtsamt für das Versicherungswesen: German Federal Insurance Supervisory Authority
BEUC (Fr)	Bureau Européen des Unions de Consommateurs: the European grouping of consumer organisations
BIS	Bank for International Settlements
CCC	Consumer Consultative Council: advisory body to the European Commission, formerly Consumer Consultative Committee
CEA (Fr)	European Insurance Committee: trade organisation of insurers
CEC	Commission of the European Communities
CECG	Consumers in the European Community Group: umbrella body for 29 UK organisations concerned

	with the effect of EC policies and proposals on UK consumers
CEN (Fr)	European Committee for Standardisation: covers EC and EFTA (q.v.)
CENELEC (Fr)	European Committee for Electrotechnical Standardisation: covers EC and EFTA (q.v.)
CEPT (Fr)	European Conference of Postal and Telecommunications Administrations
CNIL (Fr)	Commission Nationale de l'Information et des Libertés: French statutory body responsible for implementing data protection and privacy legislation
CoE	Council of Europe: intergovernmental organisation of 25 countries, including all EC member countries
COFACE (Fr)	Confederation of Family Organisations in the European Community
COREPER (Fr)	Committee of Permanent Representatives: member countries' ambassadors to the EC
CPC	Consumer Policy Committee of OECD (q.v.)
CPS	Consumer Policy Service of the European Commission: formerly part of DG XI, but now a separate service
DG	Directorate-General: one of 23 departments of the European Commission, each with a Roman numeral as suffix – for example, DG XV is the Directorate-General for Financial Institutions and Company Law
EBA	ECU Banking Association
EBF	European Banking Federation
EC	European Community/ies: entity of 12 member countries which have signed the Treaties establishing the European Coal and Steel Community, the European Atomic Energy Community and the European Economic Community
ECJ	European Court of Justice: responsible for the uniform interpretation of EC law
ECOSOC	Economic and Social Committee: Committee of the EC representing employer, trade union and other interests, whose members are nominated by governments

ECU	European Currency Unit: a unit of account (but not as yet a currency) whose value is calculated according to a weighted average of European currencies: on 29 July 1991, one ECU was worth just under 70p in sterling (1 ECU=£0.6992)
EEC	European Economic Community; one of the three original European Communities constituting the EC
ECSA	European Credit Sector Associations: comprising three banking organisations – European Banking Federation, Savings Bank Group of the EEC and Association of Co-operative Banks of the EC
ECPS	European Council for Payment Systems: grouping of banking organisations involved in providing payment systems
EFT	Electronic Funds Transfer: the direct transfer of funds from one bank account to another using electronic means
EFTA	European Free Trade Association: grouping of six countries which have free trade arrangements amongst themselves and economic links with the EC – Austria, Finland, Iceland, Norway, Sweden and Switzerland
EFTPOS	Electronic Funds Transfer at Point-of-Sale: a method of obtaining authorisation for payment and guaranteeing the transfer of funds by electronic means from the consumer's account with a bank or other financial institution to the retailer's account
EMS	European Monetary System: system whose objective is the stabilisation of exchange rates
EMU	Economic and Monetary Union: common economic and monetary policies
ERM	Exchange Rate Mechanism: linkage of EMS (q.v.) currencies through a core exchange rate for each currency, subject to a narrower or wider margin of fluctuation
ESCB	European System of Central Banks: proposed EC institution with responsibility for monetary policy – variant of Eurofed (q.v.)
ETSI	European Telecommunications Standards Institute
ETUC	European Trades Union Confederation

EUROCOOP	European Community of Consumer Co-operatives
Eurofed	Proposed EC central bank – variant of ESCB (q.v.)
FIMBRA	Financial Intermediaries, Brokers and Managers Regulatory Association: UK Self-Regulatory Organisation or SRO (q.v.)
IBRD	International Bank for Reconstruction and Development
IMF	International Monetary Fund
INTAMIC	International Association for Microcircuit Cards
IOB	Insurance Ombudsman Bureau: UK non-statutory complaints and redress body
IOCU	International Organisation of Consumers Unions
ISO	International Standards Organisation
LAUTRO	Life Assurance and Unit Trust Regulatory Organisation: UK Self-Regulatory Organisation or SRO (q.v.)
MEP	Member of the European Parliament
NVVK (Nl)	Municipal Credit System
OECD	Organisation for Economic Co-operation and Development: intergovernmental grouping of 24 industrialised countries
OJ	*Official Journal*: official community publication
ONP	Open Network Provision: framework for interoperability of telecommunications networks and services
PIN	Personal Identification Number: allocated by a bank or other financial institution for use with a payment card in an ATM (q.v.) or EFTPOS (q.v.) terminal
SCHUFA (Ger)	Protective Association for General Credit Precautions: German federation of credit reference agencies
SEA	Single European Act or Single Act
SIB	Securities and Investments Board: UK umbrella Self-Regulatory Organisation or SRO (q.v.)
SICAF (Fr)	Société d'Investissement à Capital Fixe: French collective investment fund with fixed capital
SICAV (Fr)	Société d'Investissement à Capital Variable: French collective investment fund with variable capital

SRO	Self-Regulatory Organisation: UK body recognised on the basis of statutory requirements set out in the Financial Services Act 1986
TEG (Fr)	Taux Effectif Global – see APR
UCE (Sp)	Union de Consumidores de España: Spanish consumer organisation
UCITS	Undertakings for Collective Investment in Transferable Securities: open-ended investment funds including unit trusts and other mutual funds

Index